Over Rainbow Bridge

This book is a GIFT to the Anacortes Library. Please circulate.

Diana Lola Caple

To request permissions, contact
Caple Enterprises at (360) 466-4720

Paperback: 9780578950150
Library of Congress Control Number: 2021914158
First paperback edition December 2021.

Edited by Diana Caple
Cover photograph by Diana Caple
Layout by Chelanne Evans

Printed in the USA by Village Books, Bellingham, WA.
1-800-392-2665

Titles in Alphabetic Order

Accidental Friends

Pete and I retired in 1996 and headed South in January to find the sunshine. We were leaving behind the cold, wet, depressing dark days of the Northwest to enjoy a fresh start in Tucson, Arizona. Longing for new hobbies and adventures we settled into a lovely two bedroom apartment on the ninth hole at the Ventena Resort in East Tucson.

While lounging idly one day at our local swimming pool, we met another newly retired couple, Bob and Geri Neidermiller. The last name alone should have caused us to question this acquaintance but we were eager to make new friends. Bob and Geri had another home in Detroit, Michigan and were renting an apartment close to the pool so we chatted about all the usual boring retirement topics and found we had quite a bit in common - boating, golfing, love of fast cars, and a shaky newness to the retirement life. We had all been managers and Type A personalities so getting along and deciding who was planning what became a challenge. Bob usually won out because he was the loudest and most obnoxious. Sometimes we stopped making suggestions just so he would shut up.

Geri and I knew this would be a good thing for us, as the boys would spend time on the golf range and give us the free time we so richly deserved. We also instantly knew we would have some adjustments getting to know one another. Geri had that overly-bleached blonde hard as nails look and a shipyard vocabulary to match. I wasn't a naive person as I had worked daily in the rough, tough world of teen-age delinquents but I did have a superior cultivated vocabulary. Geri reminded me a little of some of the tougher kids I had to deal with. The use of the "shit" word was everyday use to her, among many other colorful sexual shockers. This wasn't a very likely friendship but we were desperate to get rid of our husbands for at least one day a week, maybe even two, so we became pals.

Bob, a heavy set muscular six foot two, was a contrast to Pete's skinny six foot two - Mutt and Jeff came to mind. Off they went to the driving range one day with their World War Two, hand-me-down clubs, to test their strength. They were as rusty as their clubs. But never-mind, Geri and I had a free day and all we had to do was learn to get along.

We spent our first day together hiking in Sabino Canyon. Geri talked the whole time, complaining mostly about Bob, and then any person she could think of. I began to understand this catty attitude was simply entertainment to her and perhaps a Detroit tough talk survival skill. I was hoping she wouldn't talk about me the way she did about her so-called friends. Geri had been a corporate manager for Chrysler in Detroit and did the troubleshooting between service department and clients. She could call a spade a spade and put people in their place with a glance of those narrow blue eyes, brassy look, and colorful language. I was quite a contrast with my shy demeanor, overly Emily Post manners, and curly natural grey hair. Geri could have eaten me for lunch, spit me out, and run over me with one of her four-wheel drive trucks. Something about Geri made me stay on board with this beginning friendship as I decided to make this a challenge, instead of retreating to a good book or a Betty Davis movie. At least she talked to me - that was something. Pete had always been too quiet a person, a deep fountain without the deepness.

Geri eventually let me talk too, especially after I learned to just jump in and not wait for an opening. She told great jokes about just almost anything and though somewhat crass in nature, the humor was great. An example: "An old man asked his wife, what ever happened to our sexual relation? She replied, I don't know, I didn't even see him at Christmas?"

When we got bored with our hiking and swimming, we took classes together at the Senior Center. Later we joined an art class and spent one day a week drawing, painting and chatting with other women. We were such an unlikely couple, the loud-mouthed brassy blonde from Detroit and the quietspoken prissy from LaConner. "Prissy" and "Fussy" were two names Geri liked to call me. Geri was impatient – high energy, I was slow paced and overly organized. "Get off the dime! We don't have all day," she would bark at me. Well, of course, we became close friends and still are. Although we ended up living in difference states we still have a friendship and I know next time I'm in Tucson, Geri will pick me up at my hotel and we will go for lunch and she will tell me everything that's happening and we will laugh and laugh. We are lifetime friends and that is as good as it gets.

The Age of Innocence

As a child growing up in the 40's and 50's I saw my world as protective and innocent. There were many boundaries setup for me by my parents, school and society. As a female I took care of people which for me included my family of eight. I was always doing chores for my parents and babysitting my siblings, feeling useful and happy in my role. Contributing to my family kept me busy and feeling important as early as age four and as late as now at my current age of 64.

Innocence in the 40's and 50's was a very small defined space. I was a child with childhood responsibilities; I was not expected to be an adult until age 16. I knew the adults in my life had to handle all the major events and tragedies and I trusted all the adults in my life - my parents, my teachers, my neighbors, and my government. If the cold war was coming, I could hide under my desk, feel safe, and let the government and army take care of the big stuff.

I grew up as an outdoors child in a small town. All children had the run of their neighborhoods and roamed freely from property to property. My playground was the entire town and everyone seemed to know me. No one locked their doors at night. Neighbors looked after each other and healthy behavior was well defined and expected. "Yes Sir" and "No Mam" were common replies from child to adult. The only controversial conversation going on in Baudette, Minnesota was between the women sitting around the coffee table. The four party phone line occasionally brought some juicy gossip but there was no television, no cell phone, no internet, and definitely not much connection between towns. The age of innocence in Baudette was also an age of ignorant bliss. My parents never discussed world tragedies around the dinner-table because for the most part we didn't know what was happening. Our conversations centered around our neighborhood events - who was going on vacation and where, and the latest dance at the local Moose Hall.

One might ask how I escaped the age of innocence and the age of ignorance and that is a complex question. Perhaps Geographic change and the addition of hi-tech tools impacted my thinking. I think that is true. I also looked around my family and saw aunts and uncles with doctorate degrees. The aunts in my family, although well-educated, still did not work outside the home. My Grandfather and Uncles had doctorate degrees, taught college classes and had deep intellectual conversations with after dinner pipes and cigars in the parlor where the women were not allowed. I also saw my mother struggling to care for six children, still smoking her cigarettes around her coffee table and not pursuing education or a college career. God had given me a high IQ and strong motivation and I knew from a young age that I could achieve more than my mother or father if I wished to.

With the major event of television into our home, I learned that Lucille Ball was a funny witty lady, that Gracie was scatter brained but still smart, that Bette Davis had great English diction, and Lana Turner used sex to get her men and riches. I was finally exposed to the world and all my choices for myself started to open up. Television taught me that I could be any person I wanted to be. I could still be a homemaker like my mother but I could also have a career. After all, Mary Tyler Moore was working and discussing her ideas with her boss. I felt angry that men were dominating careers and government. I saw the lack of opportunities for women at an early age and am still angry about this today.

When the 60's arrived individualism replaced conformity and the age of innocence was disappearing. Experimentation in everything from sex, drugs and future thoughts was taking place at all work places and on all the colleges and universities. People like myself who grew up in the 40's and 50's were ripe for release from the boundaries. Even a female could have the same choices as men and what a threshold that was - like diving off the edge of a cliff, not knowing if one would land on water or rocks. And nobody cared. Living for the moment was all that counted. The age of innocence was replaced by a lack of traditional values and the branches from the tree drifted willingly into unknown territory. This was an exciting time to be a woman.

Andrea and Andrew

This is a strange true story to tell but definitely worth the telling. During the 1980's I was the principal of an Alternative School for high school dropouts, located in Renton, Washington. I was use to the re-entry and transfer students who came from a variety of backgrounds and difficulties. Teen parents, drug and alcohol rehabs, underage criminals on probation, failures from a traditional learning system, and special needs adults, ages 18 to 21. The other principals in the Renton School system loved my school because it gave them a place to refer a student who didn't fit into their school or was causing too many problems with the other students. So I got the referral phone call, did an evaluation, and placement into a different type of classroom where a student could achieve. This was a controlled learning environment with one-on-one help from a teacher, experienced in individualized assessment and lots of TLC. The class met for a morning or afternoon, four hours a day, with one teacher. All subjects were taught by the same teacher. So basically the student was required to get along with one teacher instead of the usual six or seven at the high school. Our success rate with drop outs and referrals was eighty percent.

Again I say this is a strange true story to tell but definitely worth the telling. One day I received a call from Catherine, the high school counselor at Renton High School. She had a student to refer to our school, but wanted me to know the situation so I could say yea or nay - all confidential information of course. "Andrea," she said, is in our science honors program. She is not a problem student but the other students in the building are being mean to her and the level of teasing is reaching the cruel and unbearable stage. Due to a series of surgeries, yet to take place, Andrea will be changing into Andrew. She has the support of her parents for the gender change operations but her teenage peers are not so supportive. You will understand more after meeting with her. Her depression is getting worse and we feel she might bolt if we don't move her into another school. She is a very bright student but needs a different environment while she proceeds into a he.

I told Catherine I would mull this over and call her back. This was a first for me and I needed time to digest the problem and think about how this would impact the students in my building. Most alternative-type teens were very accepting of the individuals who "march to a different drum." Being odd and different at my school was the norm. But would Andrea into Andrew be acceptable to our students. And what about the teachers and all their questions and jokes. Teenagers had lots of concerns about sexuality issues as the hormones were surging through their bodies like unfocused lava spouting from the volcano. I had learned to counsel the gay teenagers in my building and had some experience with the "coming out of the closet" group. We were a small community school where secrets and gossip became daily conversation.

After three days of mulling, I started to come to a conclusion. I had a leadership role in the building and this was certainly outside my experience realm. I couldn't look on page 95 of my behavior modification book and advise the teacher about what might work for this student. Also, I had visions of transvestites circling my head; those humorous Los Vegas acts that were pure entertainment for me. I wouldn't want those folks in my building. The more I mulled, the more negative I felt. I decided my answer would be NO; someone else in the district would have to take care of Andrea. This was the month of November and the teachers had finally achieved an "even keel" in their classrooms which certainly made my job easier. September had been the usual overtaxing month with lots of new enrollment. October had been "throw the bums out" month so the students that really wanted to learn could have a safe, controlled environment. November was the "tired as hell" month for the teachers and myself. We needed the simple problems at this point - not the bizarre.

Catherine was my favorite high school counselor and we traded favors; she would be hard to say NO to. I think she sensed my nervousness and uncertainty and didn't wait for my mulling to stop. Catherine called to say, "I sent Andrea to your office for an interview and seeing her will help you make up your mind." When Andrea arrived, I was taken back by her (excuse me!) his appearance. No one would think this person was a girl. And more obvious to me was the fact that this person probably didn't like being a girl. Short black haircut gathered under a ball cap, well worn blue jeans, and a white buttoned shirt resting on a flat chest, no makeup and large husky shoulders. I realized instantly that no one would take her appearance for Andrea. Andrew would be the fitting name for sure. She-he was polite and articulate about subject matter that I felt shy about. She wanted to start our school as soon as possible to avoid the stares and meanness of her peers. "They don't understand what I am going through," she said. Neither did I, I thought to myself. Looking into her deep troubled blue eyes I said, "Yes, next Monday would be fine," and I called Catherine and told her everything was a GO. Catherine assured me that Andrea would be a delight to have around. Easy for her to say, I thought to myself.

The next Monday Andrea arrived with other new students for orientation, the usual paperwork fill-outs, explanation of rules for the building, and the gentle walk to the classroom to meet the teacher. I had chosen Tim for Andrea because Tim had a no nonsense approach in his classroom where teasing others would not be tolerated. Also he preferred not to have the background information on a student; figuring things out for himself was his preference. At the morning break, snack time for students, Andrea's teacher Tim, walked into my office and closed the door behind him, "Okay, Diana, tell me the truth is my new student a he or a she?" He had a natural curiosity that most people would have after meeting Andrea, so I told him the situation and why she-he was here. Tim, like me, had dealt with the strangest of teens and this was his first experience with gender transfer also. He next asked me, "What bathroom is she going to use?" "Which ever one she or he prefers, I replied. "If it doesn't become a problem, let's not make it one now. Let's see how things go. I'm mostly concerned about the level of teasing so keep alert to Andrea's feelings. She doesn't need the extra stress, which is why she is here." Tim gave me the look that said "I don't know if this is going to work in my classroom" and reluctantly went back to class.

The happy ending to this story is that Andrea, after six months of off and on surgery, asked people to start calling her Andrew. Before our very eyes we saw a very sad faced Andrea turn into a smiling, dark facial haired Andrew. Andrew was a charming intelligent teenager who won a scholarship to the University of Washington in Marine Biology. After attending U of W a couple of years, he came back to visit and to thank us for helping him through a difficult time in his life. I often think of this brave young man who handled a situation that most adults could not. Through the years I lost tract of him as I did of so many students, but I will never forget his face. When I see the orca whales swimming off of San Juan Island, I think of Andrew and know he too had gained the freedom to be himself.

The Attraction and Break-up

Across the room, I spied a shy, tall 6' redhead chatting with a pack of similar types in blue jeans and t-shirts. Friday night at the Canteen at the Masonic Hall in Edmonds, Washington was my favorite dancing place. The dee-jay announced a "Ladies' Choice" so I ogled around the room, looking for my next victim. There he was, looking like James Dean in my favorite movie magazine. He even had the hunch and hands in the pocket look. Bright red wavy hair was piled on top of his head, greased back with Brule Cream into a pointed duck tail. I had been warned by my wall-flower girlfriends that Pete was a wild thing, the head of a skip-out ring in high school, smoked cigarettes and had his own 1934 classic Plymouth which was seen often at the submarine races at the local drive-in. At age 16, my hormones were off balance and I was bored with the geeky types at Edmonds High School. Pete looked like perfect fun for me - anyway it was just a dance. So off I wandered right into the clicky pack of males who were deeply concentrating on the latest car-engine talk from Popular Mechanics. Like in a daze, I heard my small voice say to the tall redhead, "Would you like to dance?"

He never even spoke to me, so I turned and walked away, but to my surprise he had followed me to the dance floor. "I don't know how to do this," he whispered in my ear. "It's easy", I said, "I'll show you how to do the Camel Walk." The dee-jay had just put on a new 45 record, called "Poison Ivy." Taking my hand, standing side by side, I showed him how to rock back and forth in a stooped over position, like a pair of rocking horses. We never talked, the music was loud, and after the dance, he thanked me and quickly retreated to the safety of his male pack. I was a popular dancer and many boys whirled me around the dance floor before the night ended. I knew all the dances - the twist, the slide, the fish, the hand-jive, the monkey, the swing, and several waltz steps. I knew Pete was watching me, so I flung myself around, and onto all these other boys just so he could see what he was missing. The last half-hour of the evening was for slow dancing. Most of we teenage girls were hoping for a ride home with someone other than a parent. Sometimes I got lucky but not usually, because I had the reputation of a four-eyed geek. Most of the boys interested in me were just like me, studious and over serious about everything. Dry and boring. I was cute though, even with my glasses on, and tonight I had taken extra care with my makeup, eyelash curler, and had teased my hair into a large up-do with extra hair spray. The dee-jay was putting on the last 45 of the night, Paul Anka's, dreamy song - "Put Your Head on My Shoulder."

I felt a gentle tap on my shoulder, and there he was, Pete, with his dreamy blue whirlpool eyes, looking down at me, asking me to dance. I tried to look casual, to hesitate a bit, but my heart was racing. I was getting into unknown territory, and I was glad. "Yes." I said. Slow dancing in 1957 was very intimate. Pete certainly knew how to be intimate. He wrapped his arms around me like a bear hug. I did the same. Because he was ten inches taller than I, I couldn't put my head on his shoulder like in the song but the warmth of his chest felt just fine. His head rested on my head, our bodies were tight together and we swayed gently back and forth, occupying only a two foot square spot. I had never felt a physical attraction as deep as this one, I could hardly breathe and the silence between us took on a language that only two wantabe lovers understand. I knew I would say yes to the ride home, hoping for a good-night kiss outside my door. And, yes, I got both from Pete and a lot more but that's another story.

After the attraction at the Canteen, Pete started giving Diana rides to school everyday. After school, Pete usually ended up at Diana's house to help care for the five younger brothers and sisters. Lola, Diana's mother, was thrilled to have Pete around because Les, Diana's father, was never home. Lola and Pete quickly bonded and Pete often stayed for dinner which was usually spaghetti, hot dogs, or chili. Sometimes Diana went over to Peter's house for dinner. Myrtle, Pete's Mom, was a superior gourmet cook who often baked lamb and roast potatoes. Dinner was a formal affair at Pete's house with a cocktail hour, a salad with a choice of your favorite dressing, the main course, polite formal conversation at the dinner table, followed by a homemade desert like baked apple ala mode.

As Pete and Diana spent more and more time together, they became "Steady Eddies". Soon Diana was wearing Pete's class ring around her neck on a chain. Every student at Edmonds Senior High School knew who Diana belonged to. Girls belonged to guys back in the 50's and the popular song "A Man chases a girl until she catches him" was the way it was. We teenage girls were in pursuit of our MRS Degrees and having a steady boyfriend was a step in the right direction. Our high school was full of "Steady Eddies." I felt sorry for the wall flower types who couldn't rely on a steady date. It was comforting not to worry about a date for the Tolo or Senior Prom.

Pete's dad drove a brand new white Cadillac. My Dad drove a used Chevolet station wagon. Pete's house was at the top of a two acre lot with a view of the ocean. My house was in suburban-ville and looked the carbon of the house next door. Pete's folks raised chickens, goats, and lambs. My folks raised six children on a middle income salary. Pete's Mom, my idol, worked as a legal secretary for Lloyd's of London at the Dexter Horton building in downtown Seattle. Lola, my Mom, had no formal education and did not work outside the house. Pete was an only child and I was the oldest of six children. Despite our family differences, we seemed to enjoy each other's homes immensely. These differences helped our relationship grow as Pete adopted my loud noisy unpredictable sibblings and I adopted the formal social graces of his very English manners.

Our Steady Eddy lifestyle seemed too good to be true. We attended all the games and dances together. Pete took Diana to the drag races and football games. Diana took Pete to her Presbyterian youth group and school social clubs. Like Double-mint chewing gum, we were stuck together, glued at the hip and destined to become engaged, married, and have lots of kids. In 1960, we both graduated from high school, and started our summer jobs. Pete worked at a wrecking yard. Diana worked as a switchboard operator for Blume's Chevrolet. We were both around cars and people all day. But on the weekends we found time for each other so our love could continue to grow.

Towards the end of the summer, Pete surprised Diana with an engagement ring over dinner at the Space Needle. At age 18 and 19, we were now an engaged couple. Pete was dead sure of having Diana as his life-time wife. Diana was proud to wear the oversized diamond ring on her fmger. Lola was pleased. Myrtle was overjoyed to finally have a daughter and told me often what a good match I was for her son, Peter.

This is where this story gets quirky. While Pete had the mind set that a marriage with me was the perfect adventure for him, I had a lot of doubt creeping into my brain. I had been pinned down in a family with second mother responsibilities and had little experience with the outside world. I was very restless to explore other horizons outside my immediate environment. I wanted to jump into the unknown cow pies all by myself. I still had feelings for Peter but he seemed an obstacle to my upcoming freedom. Steady Eddy looked like Nightmare Freddy.

At the end of summer, 1960, Pete started Everett Community College, while living at home. Diana moved to Seattle into a boarding house, two blocks from the University of Washington campus. The distant between us was expanding. I was exposed to the wonders of the University District, the magic of roommates, the excitement of professors who gave lectures in gigantic auditoriums. The 1934 Plymouth that Pete used as his dating cocoon seemed obsolete to me. In November, 1960, I gently told Pete I no longer wished to be engaged and needed at least a year on my own. He reluctantly took back his ring and argued with me over what a mistake I was making. He was very upset, depressed, but I was determined. The taste of freedom was delicious to me. I wanted more of the same. We said our goodbyes. A whole year passed before we met again and that will be another story.

Our front porch, covered with frozen snow, was a storage place for snow gear and a launching pad for our toboggans. 200 feet below the porch, lay the Rainy River. Canada and Baudette shared the river. One could simply walk across the ice in the winter or swim across the river in the summer to reach Canadian shores. Canadian customs was lax in those days, a car driving across the bridge would simply honk when entering Canada and that was that. In the 1950's the river was a playfield for winter sports and the gathering spot for bonfires, skating parties, and ice fishing shacks.

One could get hurt riding on a toboggan so we had strict rules. The heaviest person rode on the back, the lightest in front where the legs could be tucked under the overboard, and no more than six people at a time. We wrapped our arms tightly around the person in front and tucked our legs around the waist of the same person. If one person fell out, we would all fall. The purpose of all this tight hugging was to insure we all stayed on the toboggan while traveling 20 mph down the hill. Off the frozen porch we would slide, sailing over three bumps on the hill and then the final launch propelled us onto the frozen river and 20 more feet into the middle of the flat snowy surface. After counting our fingers and toes, we helped pull the heavy sled back to the front porch and repeated the cycle. Children would line up, yelling,"My turn next!"

The Baudette house was a magical place to live. I was eight years old and could easily escape into one of the upstairs bedrooms, the large front or back porch, or the basement which smelled of damp drying clothes on the lines, and musty cardboard boxes. Off the basement was a 12 x 12 cellar, filled with canned fruits and vegetables. The cellar had large double doors off the basement and another set of double doors which opened up above to the summer earth outside. When mother blew her shrill whistle we children would run quickly to hide down in the cellar while a nearby tornado tore across an unpredictable spot of land, tearing down houses and carrying off the loose debris. Somehow the cats and dogs seemed to know what was going on and found their own shelter. Minnesota climate came in extremes - snow storms in the winter and tornadoes in the summer. large cardboard boxes, labeled mittens, scarves, hats, pants, tops, etc. There were six of us kids, so the boxes came in handy except when a brother or sister stole a favorite hat or scarf which happened a lot. The back porch also had a wooden clothes rack to hold wet items. With our faces frozen red, and toes no longer felt, we loved to climb into the mudroom and disassemble ourselves.

The living room was a gathering place for the whole family after dinner. The Motorola radio was a large piece of oak furniture, shaped like a jukebox with Rochester Show, Arthur Godfrey, Amos and Andy, and a scary show called Inter- sanctum which always started with a slow creaking door. To the right of the living room, a wooden staircase ascended to the second floor which held one bathroom and three bedrooms. My bedroom was the best because I had an outside lanai with double doors, which I could open to view the nighttime stars.

Mother did not have many rules about the house. Because the inside windows were frosted she advised us never to lick the window. I remember one of my mischievous brothers put his tongue on a window to taste the popsicle-like crystals and mother had to take a pot of hot water to gently remove his tongue while he cried and wiggled like an eel. The crystals on the windows were like sheets of art, differently arranged as though an artist had worked her magic.

The winter blizzards would give us cabin fever until mother brought out all the puzzles which were placed on the dining room table. We would sit on the floor in the kitchen to eat our meals so as not to disturb the puzzles. If we had a favorite puzzle, we could glue the pieces together and pin our masterpiece on our bedroom wall. I had one whole wall covered with puzzles by the end of winter.

In 1996 I took my husband, Peter, to visit the town I grew up in and to the house by the river. A new owner had just purchased the house, a lover of arts and crafts which were displayed in every room adding a cluttering feeling to the space. I thought she cluttered the space too as her large frumpy body made the doorway seem small. She was generous enough to let us into the house. I took Pete up the long stairway to show him my bedroom. The same flowery wallpaper adorned the walls but the lanai was walled- in to add another room to the house. Rainy River was full of wild rice patties which were farmed by new

Baudette immigrants. It was September; no snow on the ground, and the house seemed to belong to another time and space.

Blizzard of 1954

The snow falls in clumps on the roof. All night the wind shrieks and whistles and I know these sounds of a blizzard afoot. My bedroom window is still open and cold crisp air fills my nostrils, making it difficult to breathe. Prisms of dried flakes on the inside of the window make white patterns of lace. As my fingers touch the patterns, I feel the shivery frost stick under my nails. My breath circles above my mouth, making tug-boat steam in small circles. I am not alone in my bedroom, but I am the first one to wake to the bitter cold. Pam and Flora share the other single bed, sleeping at opposite ends. Pam has wiggly feet and Flora wets the bed sometimes so I am grateful for a bed all to myself. Being the oldest child has its privileges. I am twelve years old and this is the first time I have had a bed all to myself.

I am the second to rise. My mother, Lola, is creating cooking sounds in the kitchen; pans are sizzling with salty smells. Slipping quietly out of my blankets, I add a warm robe and a jacket and snuggle my feet into my large pink wool floppy slippers. I can feel the fibers sticking between my toes. Flopping down the hall, I revel in the smells coming from the kitchen - sausage and bacon, Folgers coffee, and Pall Mall cigarette smoke. The three brothers are still sleeping and have a separate bedroom with a mattress on the floor. As I tiptoe by, Zip, the golden retriever opens his eyes but stays put, snuggling next to my brothers. Even the dog is reluctant to leave the warm covers.

Arriving in the kitchen, I see the Coleman stove set up on the dining room table and a Coleman lantern lit in the corner. Paper plates and cups are stacked up for an easy cleanup time. In Rapid City, South Dakota, a strong blizzard will often cause the electricity to fail. Today there will be no loud noises in our house from the gadgets; the television, dishwasher, and washing machine will be mute. In the kitchen, news information is airing from the battery operated radio. "People are advised to stay indoors and conserve heat

. The snowplows are not at work yet. School has been cancelled for the day. Stay tuned for further announcements."

Mom looks cheerfully at me and says, Diana, we will have a game day with the kids today, so let's think of things to do." She loves this time of no electricity and so do I. I know today will be different from the usual day and we will be challenged to make our own entertainment.

All the children are gathered snugly around the breakfast table with anticipation of salty tastes and sweet blackberry jam. We are all too hungry and too cold to fight so we practice our happy faces. After breakfast we set up the two card tables next to the Coleman lanterns. Pam, Flora, and I find the old Sears catalogs and fashion magazines and the scissors. We will make our own paper dolls and plan travel trips for all our people creations. Next we set up the tinker toys, Cootie body parts, and Mr. Potato Head on one of the tables for the boys. All seven of us are nestled together in one room but we feel warm and safe, glad to be away from the howls and gales of the wind. My Dad is away on a trip so we must be brave and help Mom with whatever she needs. Even the brothers are on their best behavior.

The blizzard of 1954 dumps thirty inches of snow in 24 hours. Our small three bedroom rambler has snow drifts ten feet high and I feel the eerie sense of being buried in a vast white blanket. The next day our front door will not open into the packed snow, so we must climb out a window on the back side of the house, the leeward side that escapes the largest snow drifts. Pam and I open the bedroom window wide and roll our bodies sideways into the snow, like angels descending on virgin clouds. The fresh snow smells like pure bleach and shocks our noses. Pam and I unbury the snow shovels and go to work, clearing a path to the front door. Bundled up with sweaters and jackets, we are sweating from our efforts but the bright sunshine on our backs shows the promise of a warmer day.

In The Blink of An Eye

Christmas vacation, 1984, was our time to escape from the dreary dampness of Seattle weather. Pam, Pete, and Diana took turns each year planning a two week vacation at Christmas, a time they could get away from their jobs together. The only travel rule they had was the vacation had to be in a warm weather climate with a beach. Diana had chosen Ixtapa, Mexico with a high rise hotel on the beach. We had just arrived and had finished scouting along the shoreline in front of the towering hotels, checking out the pools and cabanas. We now wanted to hike the backside of the hotels and the colorful shops. It felt good to stretch our legs after the long plane ride.

Southern Mexico was new to us. The climate was much hotter and humid than we had experienced in Northern Mexico. We had stripped to our bathing suits and sandals and started drinking the extra bottled water we carried. Life was feeling extremely lazy among the palm trees and exploring the rainforest fauna was a feast for our eyes. After passing by hotels on the west end, we spied a group of condos surrounding a man-made golf course. We were on a long sidewalk adjoining the golf greens but separated by a short wooden fence. It was the middle of the day and the golf course was deserted, probably due to the intensity of the heat. The lovely green manicured grass was calling to us, so we hopped the fence to explore yet another way back to our hotel.

From a distance we could see a large statue on the ground next to a twenty foot ditch, still part of the golf course. Soon Pam let out a cry, "Wow! Do you see that alligator - looks almost real." "No, Diana replied, "There's no alligators in Mexico, probably another sculpture by a local artist." As we got closer and closer, the statue seemed to be in a deep sleep, eyes closed with leather like lids, and a mouth agape with artistically enameled spiked teeth. We stood close by and admired the amazing skill of the artist. Quite a large sculpture, six feet in length, large webbed leather toes, a snaky skin with mixed colors of green, brown, and grey. We knew from our experience that animals too hot would often sleep with their mouths open to create the air ventilation that cooled their bodies. What a peaceful magnificent art form to find on the golf course. Then Pete started teasing us. "Don't get too close, it might bite. Could be the real thing." Pam and I laughed and moved closer, thinking we might touch the rough texture of the leather-like skin. Then one eye blinked. Pete said, "Did you see that." Yes, we had and we were moving slowly backwards to the golf path. We were still not sure if this lifelike statue was real or fake, but we all decided to err on the side of safety so we headed for the gate which would lead us back to the beach. When we opened the gate, we saw a large warning sign that said, "Beware of the alligators!" Thank god our alligator statue wanted his nap more than a snack.

Boats, Yachts, and Ships
(The Early Years)

Pete's first job at age 14 began his career with boats, yachts, and ships. Haines' Fishing Wharf was located in Meadowdale, Washington where Pete lived with his mom, Myrtle, and dad, Hoyt. Haines' Wharf was a half mile walk down a steep hill to the waterfront named Puget Sound. One hundred wooden boats, 16' to 21,' and motors were available to rent. The small motors were Mercury's and the largest motor was named after Bill Muncy, the hydro-plane driver. Haines also had a tackle shop which stocked all the needs of the fishermen. Pete's main job was to clean the boats upon return, hosing out the blood and fish guts, and wiping down the outside, so the boat was then ready for the next renter. His favorite part of this summer job was lowering the boats into the water by use of a hand operated brake and clutch that was driven by a Model B Ford engine. When the boats returned, especially in rough currents and wind, the process had to be timed just right to catch the boat onto the elevator floor and he loved the challenge. Pete loved the fishy, salty smells of the waterfront and the comradery of the other men. Haines' Wharf also caught herring off the dock by lowering a cage into the water with a spot light attached. Herring would be attracted to the light and then caught in the trap. Pete's job was to empty the traps and package the herring for sale to the fishermen. One day a young man bet Pete a dollar that he couldn't eat a live herring. "Game on," replied Pete. But, as the herring was too wiggly inside his throat, he spat it out. Attempt failed. The other man picked up a herring, snapped it on the head with his fingers, and swallowed it whole. Not one to lose a dollar, Pete grabbed another herring, snapped it on the head, and down it went. "Now we are even," he said.

Pete's Dad had a 42 foot wooden Chris-Craft with twin inboard engines, so Pete spent many days yachting in the Puget Sound, San Juan Islands, and up north into Canada. During these boat trips, Pete was allowed to steer the boat and help his Dad with engine repairs. Painting, waxing the wood, changing the oil, and other skills were all taught by his Dad, who had spent 30 years in the Coast Guard and had current knowledge of the marine industry. Pete loved the boat bonding time with his Dad. His Mom, called "little chicken" by his Dad, was the best galley cook ever.

Towards the end of one of their trips in the Canadian Islands, Pete was dropped off in Vancouver, B.C. to catch the train home. School was about to start and his parents wished to continue their cruising up North by themselves. When Pete tried to pass through Canadian Customs, the custom officers were not pleased. He was a minor, age 16, traveling alone with illegal papers. His parents had photocopied his birth certificate to a wallet size. Pete also had a current driver's license but because he had been born in England, the custom officers wanted proof of citizenship and naturalization papers. Pete said, "You can call my parents." "Indeed we will, the officer said, but meantime we will let you board the train home." The train in those days stopped in Meadowdale by Haines' Wharf so Pete was able to walk up the hill to home. Two weeks later his Dad got a call from a Custom's Officer, who chewed him out for doing something illegal. Hoyt was a Lt. Commander in the Coast Guard at this time, but all he said was, "Yes,Sir."

During the summertime Pete worked for the Washington State State Ferries, ages 16 and 17. The first summer he hated the job as he was the clean-up person who swept the popcorn and other junk passengers left behind. The Enetat Ferryboat, built in 1927, cruised from Mukilteo to Clinton and back. Enetat (en-a-tie) is an Indian word that means "across, on the other side." So each hour the clean-up was done while cars were boarding and unloading. He was encouraged by his employers to "stick it out," everyone had to start at the bottom in those days. The following summer he was assigned to the engine room and he loved this job. He helped with a variety of engine repairs - oil changes, piston changes, and general maintenance on the hugh engine 6 cylinder diesel engine, 15' high by 30' wide.

During this summer of 1958, Pete also worked on the Crosline Ferryboat which did the crossings on Hood Canal. This vessel was a back-up ferry for use when a Seattle ferry broke down. The ferryboat engines were difficult to control during docking time as the engine had to be completely shut down before changing gears. Pete remembers a trip in Hood Canal when the current was rough. He was looking out from the upper deck as the Crosline approached the landing. The ferry was surging rapidly towards the pilings. The skipper shut off the engine but was unable to start the engine and put the ferry into reverse. From his perch above he saw the people on shore run for higher ground and the passengers below getting ready to disembark ran backwards towards the cars and the stairs. The Crosline hit the dolphins hard, the damage was severe, but no one was hurt. The older men taught him everything they knew about repair on the 1927 to 1950 vessels and by age 18, Pete, had advanced mechanical skills and a working knowledge of boats, yachts, and ships that would span his entire career.

Boats, Yachts, and Ships
(The Midddle Years)

After high school, Pete applied for jobs at Washington State Ferries, Blackball Line Cargo Ships, and Todd's Shipyard. His parents were encouraging him to start a four-year apprenticeship as an outside machinist. Learning a trade and joining a union was the right step towards a secure future in the 1960's. Pete was eventually hired by Todd's Shipyard where he did complete a trade as an outside machinist and stayed in the ship building business for 35 years. During this time at Todd's Pete married Diana in 1963 and moved to Freemont, Seattle. Diana also worked in Seattle at the Bon Marche as a keypunch operator and they were able to commute back and forth together.

Pete loved working on the various ships at Todd's - building and maintaining ferry vessels, cargo ships, Navy ships, and other large vessels that came to Todd's drydocks for repair. Serving an apprenticeship meant low pay. Pete's first paychecks were forty dollars a week. Items were cheap in those days and money went along way. For a quarter, you could buy a loaf of bread, go to a movie (popcorn was 10 cents), and pay 60 cents a gallon for gas. In his first four years at Todd's Pete learned the following skills about onboard ship building and repair: maintenance of steam turbines and diesel engines, installing bearings, machining foundations, and fitting propellers. The new construction of Navy destroyers included ordinance work, assembly of gear mounts, missile launchers, and stern tubes.

One day while working inside a Navy supply ship (AOE) on a reduction gear, an accident occurred. Pete was working 30 feet down the same hole that cranes were lowering equipment up and down. Somehow someone knocked over a chair, a steel swivel chair, into the hole overhead. The chair hit Pete in the face and torn part of his nose and lip away from his face and took out a tooth. At the hospital, the doctors stitched him up and sent him home. Next Monday he reported to work, but Todd's sent him home for a week off with pay. Later he received a 350 dollar check for his facial disfigurement.

Dave Brown was the foreman of the outside machine shop and Pete's boss and teacher during his apprenticeship. His personality was a challenge to Pete. As a task master, his words were often off-color and unclear. He only gave basic instruction and then would walk away. So Pete found comfort in the notebooks that described how to do each job. Pete felt ignored and was stuck with repetitive jobs. At the end of his apprenticeship he asked for a six month extension and a new instructor. He was assigned to the inside machine shop with a new foreman Walt Ifencougher. During this time Pete worked on dam gates for the Columbia River. After switching to night shift, he continued working on inside machinery.

In 1965, United States was at war in Viet Nam. Pete collected the mail one day and opened an unexpected letter - a draft notice. He was age 24, but the army recruiters were running out of live bodies and were now drafting young men who had no children. What a shock to receive that letter. Hundreds of young men were coming home in body bags toward the end of this hopeless war so Pete tried to find another armed service that would take him besides the Army. The Navy would take him, but only if he signed up for four years so he did. On his way to boot camp in California, a meningitis outbreak cancelled his boot camp and he was sent, instead, to the Great Lakes training camp in Michigan. After boot camp, Pete was assigned to the USS Destroyer Charles S. Sperry to work in the engine room. The Sperry was 376 feet long and carried a crew of 300. The Navy was taking full advantage of Pete's three years of machinist skills. During these four years, the Sperry was stationed in many ports around the world, Bahrain, Saudi Arabia, Mosinbeak, Africa, Rota, Spain, the Caribbean Islands, Puerto Rico, and stateside Pete was stationed mostly at Newport, Rhode Island and for repair work, at Boston, Massachusetts. Diana worked as a keypunch operator at Providence, Rhode Island and Newport Naval Base. Most of these years were spent apart as Pete's ship traveled for long months, sometimes 6 to 9 months at a time. During Pete's Navy years, he learned the operation of a steam turbine engine - throttle watch, evaporator watch, repairing pumps, and valves. He entered the Navy as a Fireman and left as a Second Class Petty Officer. Many re-up bribes were offered such as a $20,000 check but Pete's answer was "No." When Pete left the Navy to return to Seattle, he took additional baggage - a four month old baby named Susan Lynn, born January 17, 1969 at the Newport Naval Hospital.

Boats, Yachts, and Ships
(The Later Years)

When Pete retired, he pursued new hobbies to keep occupied. Diana still had three years left on her retirement plan. Pete liked house projects, especially carpentry, so when their 14 year renters moved out of 1055 Union Ave., Renton, WA. Pete started the remodel. The house needed a lot of work - Pete started with new sheet rock and painted the interior and exterior. When he finished 1055 looked brand new and was sold on the market in 1994, for 125,000 dollars. We had paid 25,000 dollars for this house in 1971, so a nice profit was made. But now, Pete needed another project, as Diana was still working. In 1993, Pete had inherited his Mother's house in

Shelter Bay so he and Diana decided to sell the large family house in Renton, 4000 sq. feet and make 271 Elwha their permanent home. Diana lived in an apartment by Lake Washington, walking distant to her job at the Sartori School. Meanwhile Pete started renovating the LaConner house, starting with new appliances for the kitchen. Diana commuted to Shelter Bay on the weekends. This lifestyle was not a favorite but Diana had only one year left to complete the required hours for the retirement plan she wanted from Washington State.

On December 20th, 1996, Diana retired. Renton School District hired an interim principal to replace her for the rest of the year. Now Pete and Diana could live in one place, Shelter Bay. With both of them out of work, they needed new hobbies to keep busy. Diana suggested they buy a boat and join the Shelter Bay Yacht Club. Pete's first reaction was quite negative. "Do you know how much work a boat can be? I have been around ships and boats all my life. I use to get paid for repairing boats. Besides, my Dad used to say, "Owning a boat is like throwing money down a hole." Diana really wanted a boat, she loved being out on the water, liked to fish and swim and Shelter Bay was a huge boating community. So they bargained back and forth and decided to start with a small 24 foot Trophy as a trial to see if they liked boating together. Pete wanted the latest electronic equipment so he could navigate through the islands safely with a GPS and computerized navigation system. He also warned Diana that there would be times when they would get caught in bad weather despite best efforts to do otherwise. Diana wasn't worried; she was a good swimmer and always wore her life-vest even when on the local docks.

So their boating life began and continued until the year 2000 when they sold their final boat, a 34' bayliner, with a fly bridge, named "Coralee" after Pete's grandmother Cora. Also, these last few years from 1996 to 2001, Pete and Diana spent their winter months in Tucson, Arizona. Not a bad life!- yachting trips in the summers and hiking the mountains of Arizona in the winters. These were busy happy times.

The Book-lady

Hi! My name is Sharon Leigh Caple. I am 37 years old and I live in the small eastern town of Cle Elum, Washington. My mother, Diana, asked me what my greatest accomplishment has been and I said my book collection and my reputation as the Book-lady of Cle Elum. Books are my life and surround me everywhere. I think of my antique books as good friends like my three cats, Sunflower, Lioness, and Krammer.

My love of books has spilled over into the community of Cle Elum. I live in an apartment above Pioneer Coffee Roasting Company. My sister, Susan, and ex brother-in-law started the coffee business downstairs in 2001. I moved into the building in 2001 to help them with the business. I painted walls and furniture, lugged bags of coffee beans to the roaster, learned how to be a barista and was a constant cheerful unpaid employee and go-fer. But my most important contribution to Pioneer Coffee was and still is the maintenance of the used bookstore I developed for the customers that frequent the coffee house. All the books I collect are for sale, except the occasional signed first editions that I keep for myself. The hardbacks go for five to ten dollars each and the paperbacks are two to five dollars each. Purchase of a book is on the honor system as I have a· piggy bank sitting by the bookcases that collects the money as people browse and choose a favorite book to read. I collect children's books which I give away free. I enjoy watching the children browse through my wicker baskets of books and then I tell them, "You can take a book home with you to keep." A smile broadens their faces and I hope I have helped a child become a lover of books, like me.

When I am not collecting books from garage sales, libraries, and thrift stores, I am reading books. Also, at the coffee house, I am available for book discussions and often can match the person to the right book for him or her. Sometimes a person will ask me to keep an eye out for a certain book or subject matter. The old miners in Roslyn collect books about mining and the local artists are looking for vintage art books. My Mom likes to read large print books about history and poetry. My Dad looks for the best sellers so I always have a new mystery for him to read. Sometimes

I sell a used book, then get it back and sell it again. Many local community people bring me books when they clean out their attic or bookshelves. Parents bring me their old children's books because they know I will recycle them to other children for free.

The only problem I have with my book collection is that I have run out of storage room. My very small studio apartment is full of books that I cannot part with. Books are mixed into my clothes closets, under my bed, in the kitchen cupboards. I love all this clutter of books but I will soon have to rent another apartment just for my books - Ha! People who live in clutter like me don't mind a cluttered apartment, but some people are uncomfortable with piles of books and three cats roaming around in and out of my shelves. I so wish others would appreciate and understand me better. I have a favorite movie called "84 Charing Cross Road about a woman who loves books and collects books and also lives in clutter. I recently gave this movie to my parents to watch and we all had a great laugh over Anne Bancroft as the Book-lady and Anthony Hopkins as the owner of a bookstore in London. A must see movie for all book lovers.

To me, books are constantly floating around in my crowded brain and people are always amazed at my memory retention for details from each book I have read. I only collect quality vocabulary books - books that teach and describe, educate or tell an amazingly good story. And I always have plenty of classics on my shelves. Every classic I buy finds a new owner. But sometimes I can't part with it, like my first edition of Jane Eyre, leather bound. Enough, enough, about my books. Time to go upstairs and have a good read.

The Boss

Doctor Delight had a silly name but no one teased her because she was the boss. She had a bright calculating brain which was useful to her career. Graduating from the University of Washington with a Doctorate in Statistical Science, she was the only woman in her field in the Northwest. She lived on Bainbridge Island on a twenty-acre horse ranch where she raised quarter horses for show.

I first met Dr. Delight at a job interview. Mine! Renton Vocational Technical College, formerly named RVTI, had advertised for a part-time teacher in the Learning Center. I had previously lost two jobs in the 1970's due to school enrollment decline; one at the Seattle School District, the second at Highline School District. I had been use to long drives from Renton to work. I was hoping to work close by so I could spend more time with my young children. RVTC was a mile from my house in Renton Highlands. This would be my first job with adults at a college. At this time I only had a B.A. in English Literature and a K-12 Teaching Certificate.

I had dressed neatly for my job interview and brought with me a carefully typed resume. As I entered Dr. Delight's office, my eyes swiftly took in the large, untidy woman. Overly stacked books perched hazardously on her cluttered desk. "Please take a seat," she said as she glanced at her over-sized man watch with the large digital numbers. Her dress was from the early 1960's - a half-tucked in white blouse, a large ballooning skirt to mid-calf, slip-on sandals, no jewelry, and no makeup. Her rigid frown spoke volumes and her marine blue eyes looked around me and over me. I felt very small in my pin-striped grey suit. The room smelled faintly of human sweat and barnyards. The interview lasted less than ten minutes. She glanced at her watch again, dismissed me, and was ready for the next person. Two days later I got a call from RVTC's personnel office offering me a part-time evening job, Monday, Wednesday, and Friday from 6 -9 p.m. Evening work was not what I wanted and the pay was only $12.00 per hour with no benefits. I took the job.

I didn't see much of Dr. Delight after that, because she worked days. Sometimes she would stay late to check on the evening crew and have a staff meeting where she always told us what she didn't like and gave us advice on how to get better results. Never any praise, just criticism. We all knew teachers were a dime a dozen in those days so we all worked hard and put in extra hours grading papers at home. The Learning Center served the needs of the college, so we taught the GED test, English to English as the Second Language students (ESL), individual tutoring to help students learn math, English, and reading. I had previously managed high school students so the work was easy. The students were respectful and glad to be there. The only difficulty I had was getting along with Dr. Delight. She was a bull-dozer boss who fired people. She had a short fuse for people who didn't look productive or wasted her time by asking questions.

After three months on the evening shift, I was switched to days and worked Monday through Friday in the afternoons. There was a much larger group of students and teachers on the day shift. Dr. Delight was in and out of the Learning Center and the work place was an atmosphere of seriousness and results. I missed the casual climate of the evening shift. Then the worst thing happened, Dr. Delight took a personal interest in me and decided to parade me around to her committee meetings where I would sit, nod, smile and agree to everything she said. Committee meetings were led by the college president, Dr. Roberts, and attended by whomever he summoned like the finance director, counselors, or department heads. When we attended meetings at RVTC, I saw this bull-dozer woman at work with her peers. She always brought her briefcase, and when in disagreement with a peer, she would reach into her briefcase and pull out a sheet of statistical information that toasted her opponent. I never saw her lose an argument.

Eventually I felt bored with my part-time job, so like most teachers in the 1980's I went back to college to work on a master's degree. Dr. Delight was interested in my career and would call me into her office to talk about my current classes in Special Education. She was an important asset to me when I started my statistical classes. My final year at Seattle Pacific University, I did my internship at the Renton Alternative High School and RVTC allowed me to vary my work hours so I could complete my Master's work. When I started the tedious task of statistical analyzes for my master's thesis, Dr. Delight was both my critic and supporter. My thesis was about the South King County high school dropout population, why this problem was increasing, and what were the exact reasons as told from the drop-out students' point of view.

One day to my surprise, Delight (we were now on a first name basis), called me into her office and closed the door. "Diana, I have an idea, and want you to hear me out. This year there will be grant money available to start new programs for at-risk youth. I would like you to accompany me to Olympia while I make the presentation for an at-risk program at the RVTC Learning Center. Please bring your statistical report with you and we will present our case together.

As I rode to Olympia with her one morning in her Mercedes Benz, the air in the car smelt strongly of barnyard muck. Books were piled so high that I knew she could not see out the back window. Our conversation was casual as she explained to me how she raised her quarter horses and attended contests all over the United States to win metals for the best of show. I looked over at this bull dozer woman fondly and was glad to be at her side.

The California Gold Rush

The Boeing 727 rested to a stop at LAX as we gazed at the asphalt and palm trees. My ears were stuffed like corks in a stopper, my knuckles were pure white, and my queasy stomach felt ready to rumble. However, the landing had been smooth so my body soon recovered to normal. We knew little about Los Angeles, except what we had seen from the freeway on a trip to Disneyland many years ago. In 1978 Pete had been offered a promotion into upper management at Todd Shipyard in San Pedro, so here we were to shop around for a house and look the situation over. We loved living in the Northwest and felt reluctant about this new adventure.

We had just purchased our first house at 1055 Union Avenue in Renton, Washington, located three blocks from Honeydew Elementary where our two daughters attended school. Pete had a twenty minute drive to work at Todd's on Harbor Island and Diana had a ten minute drive to Renton Vocational Technical Institute where she taught Adult Basic Education and GED. Our location in Renton was quite convenient. Our fenced backyard smelled of maple trees, blueberry bushes, and garden vegetables. We could feel the soft dirt between our toes when we walked through the rows of com. Our neighbors were close by in our cul-de-sac; their children were playmates to our children. We were very happy in Renton and at our jobs.

Now we were anticipating a move to LA. What a huge change for us. Todd's had flown us to LA to visit with Pete's soon to be new boss, Hans Shaffer, and to look at housing, schools and the general area of San Pedro. After locating the rental car at LAX, we lined up on the ramp for the freeway. The smell of heavy smog filled our lungs with a scent of vinegar and was so thick we could not see the sun. We drove to Todd Shipyard in San Pedro, a suburb of LA, and looked for a new home and schools. The neighborhood was mostly Hispanic, homes were built of adobe brick, and the heavy smog with the vinegar smell was still baking our senses. After talking with the locals, we were advised not to place our children in the public schools but to find a private Catholic school which was safer and did a much better job of educating.

We found a two story house we liked, twice the size of the small three bedrooms we now had in Renton and located a nearby Catholic school. Pete visited Todd's Shipyard in San Pedro and noted that most of the worker bees were Hispanic while most of the supervisors were Caucasian. He was wishing he had learned Spanish. While Pete visited the work environment, I visited the LA school district personnel office. Lots of immediate jobs were available, especially in my field of English and Basic math skills. The salary was considerably higher, but included two snags. One, I would have to spend my first two years teaching in the most illiterate schools where the greatest need was, and two, I would receive "combat" pay for working with the tougher students. The word "combat" kind of scared me but the personnel director assured me the schools were safe due to police patrol in the buildings.

After many conversations, no sunshine, lots of asphalt, and crowded neighborhoods, Pete and I climbed aboard the Boeing 727 to return to Seattle. We were quiet on our trip home, our brains too stuffed with the details of our move. Being torn in both directions, Pete's warm hand found mine, and he suggested we take a week to decide if this was what we really wanted to do. As we alit from the 727 to the tarmac, the asphalt had a fresh steamy scent like the morning dew on our new patio deck. The smell of green, grassy foliage hit our nostrils like entering a barn during haying season.

When our week of thinking was up, our answers to the move to LA were the same. No, we would not go. No to the promotion meant turning down a salary increase for Pete and a chance to move from Foreman, a union job, to Administration, a salaried management position with all the perks. Many of our relatives told us we were making a big mistake. "Saying No to a promotion was not a wise thing to do," Pete's parents said. Well, we felt we had made the best choice for us, so we went quietly and comfortably back into our daily routine.

** ** **

Six months later, Pete received the same salaried promotion at Todd Shipyard in Seattle, Washington. Five years later the San Pedro Shipyard closed due to outsourcing the jobs to Asian countries.

Chicken Little

"Put your feet on the chickens and stay in the kitchen," says Nana. Sam sips his wee blue cup. He is thirsty but not really; he likes the game of saying the word "thirsty", holding the cup "Me-self", the flow of the liquid to his mouth, the control of dumping the leftover water into Nana' wide white sink and setting the cup on the counter. Little ears like the sounds of swish, plop, and gurgle. Later we will repeat the game and then over and over several times a day. Sam is two and a half years old, saying "No" to most everything and declaring "Me-self" whenever an adult tries to do something for him.

Sam and I are watching the two large red hens roosting on my kitchen rug below the sink. The tuffs of red feathers stick up between his toes as he wiggles his feet back and forth, looking rather smug as if he has captured a favorite spot in my kitchen. I have to confess that my two chickens are not roosting but lie flat as part of a rug design that caught my eye when shopping at Fred Myers. Chickens have been a happy theme in our family. When we visit the wild turkeys in downtown LaConner, Sam calls them chickens. We are trying to get him to switch over to turkeys but he insists they're chickens.

When I think about my childhood experience with chickens, I feel both happy and sad. The "Chicken Little" story about the sky failing down, the acorn hurting her head, and the frightening mad dash through the woods to tell the king - I know I won't pass that story onto my grandson, despite the colorful characters of Henny Penny, Turkey Lurky, and Ducky Lucky. But, "My Black Hen" is a nursery rhyme worth savoring. I like the sounds of "Hickety, pickety, my black hen." On the internet, I found the verse and a picture to color, which I printed out so next time Sam and I play the chicken game in the kitchen, I can read him the poem and get the color crayons out for his two-year old scribbles.

I have a farm friend who let my children gather eggs and pet the chickens when they were little folks. My daughter, Sharon, called me last Easter to announce, "Guess what I'm Doing?" And, yes, at age thirty-six she was chasing and gathering up baby yellow chicks at a friend's farm to take to the local grocery stores to sell to parents for Easter gifts. She lives in a farming community, so I like to think the baby chicks got good homes. I think today it is against the law to dye baby chicks, but when I was a child we saw baby chicks in colorful feathers of pink, blue, and green. My father-in-law, now deceased, use to call his wife "Little Chicken" which was an endearing pet name for Myrtle, especially at dinnertime when she was serving one of her famous roast potato and lamb meals. "What a good little chicken she is!," he would say. I would not have liked being called a little chicken, but Peter calls me "beaner" sometimes and I in turn call my daughters "beaner." Why? I have no idea. No explanation. The name just caught on somewhere along the way.

Last week Pete and I hit a large pheasant on the road outside of Monroe - it died instantly and left feathers stuck in the grill. During hunting season, causing road-kill doesn't seem too evil. Thank god it wasn't a wild turkey or a chicken. I have to confess that while Sam and I are standing on the chicken rug, a juicy salty f-o-w-1 aroma is in the air. Later I will tell Sam to eat up all his chicken. At age two, he is already learning the conflicts that come from loving an animal and then eating one. The nursery rhymes never seem to deal with this dichotomy. "Rickety, pickety, my black hen, she lays eggs for gentlemen ... " Oh, dear, here is another problem - the poem continues with "gentlemen come every day, to see what my black hen does lay." I suspect that in the 1930's this poem reflects the common practice of gentlemen doing the looking and the women doing the egg gathering and cooking. The old nursery rhymes do reflect the sexist nature of their times. My Black Hen definitely has a black side to it. Perhaps I will pass on the story of "The Little Red Hen" who baked the bread, could find no one to help her, so she ate it all herself. What would be the moral value of that?

Closure

On June 20, 1993, at four o-clock in the afternoon, we arrived to a bright blue Arizona sky in Tucson. This was an emergency trip as Lola, Diana's Mom, was in hospice care at Tucson Medical Center and Pam, Diana's sister, had called two days ago to say "Mom will not last much longer. Come as fast as you can." My sister Pam and step-Dad Dallas had been caretakers to mother for the last five years, as Lola had one stroke after the other, but now they needed our help.

Tucson is hot and dry in June. We had come from Seattle, Washington and were use to a milder, rainy climate. Diana had gotten Pam's call while at work and had begun to delegate her responsibilities as building principal immediately. The teachers and students at Satori high school knew this was a sad time for Diana and they would stop by her office with a kind word of sympathy. Pete and Diana quickly made plane reservations and got to Tucson Medical Center the next day.

Walking into mother's room was a shock - the smell of death was lingering. Lola only weighed eighty pounds and her vital body functions had shut down. This last stroke had taken her speech as well. But we knew she could hear us talk so we could say the important things to her that she longed to hear. She would gesture and smile and point her fingers at various things in the room. The nurses showed us what to do and we took turns giving her water from a small sponge on a stick that was occasionally dipped in a glass of fresh water. We all wanted to do so much more for her but her frail body was moving into a final state. The nurse assured us she was no longer in pain due to a steady round of morphine shots.

My sister Pam, a recovery room nurse, had seen the various stages of dying and disease, but this was my first experience with death. With all my various college degrees, I was totally ignorant to this new experience. Being the oldest child of the family, I had many responsibilities growing up as a child and was the one who handled most of the family emergencies and I instinctively knew I would get through this with God's help. To me death was a simple journey into the hands of God. But, I felt tense and my emotions were raw on the surface. I did not want to lose my mother.

Not even to God.

By now it was ten o'clock at night and everyone was getting tired. Pam and Dallas had been there for four days caring for Mom around the clock. I told everyone to get some sleep and I would stay awake and keep Mom company. Pam went home to her bed, Pete left for the motel bed, and Dallas curled up on the cot below my Mother's bed and soon softly snored. Mom and I were alone but our hands were joined tightly as if we had but one body between us. I knew Lola had become my needy child and I had become the hovering parent.

As Mom progressed into dying stages of lesser breathing, her lungs and throat started to shut down. The nurse would come by to check on us. Sometimes the sheets would be changed and Lola would get another morphine shot. I knew I would not grow tired, I could have lasted for days holding my mother's hand, stroking her cheeks, and feeding her drops of water. Later, Pam called and was crying on the phone, "I can't bear to see her like this, she said, "I'm not coming back to the hospital. Call me when it's over." I knew she meant what she said. I didn't argue, even though I felt deserted. After all she was the nurse, not me. When the hospice nurse stopped by I said, "Pam is not coming back." The nurse looked at me with such gentle eyes and said, "Of course not, nurses can seldom see their parents die because they take care of everyone else's parents. This would be too hard for Pam and she knows she has you to rely on.

Mother's breathing had become labored, and she rose up in bed, with a croaking sound coming from her throat. I was afraid for her and ran for the nurse. Another morphine shot was given. Dallas woke up and kept a close vigil. We knew the end was close. I leaned over my mother, and said, "Mom, it's okay to let go." I was feeling the deepest sorrow in the pit of my stomach, my emotions were in conflict with each other. I didn't want my mom to suffer anymore but I didn't want her to die and be alone in the unknown abyss. Two orderlies came in the room and asked us to leave so they could change the sheets. We waited in the hall and when we returned Lola was resting peacefully, her eyes closed, but no longer breathing. The end had come.

Now I felt hardcore anger and a helplessness that came from deep in my soul. I felt the coldness of my mother's hand and I wept uncontrollable sops. In this moment I prayed to God to look after her and not let her be alone. She had raised six children, had three husbands, lots of cats and dogs and definitely didn't like to be alone. Where had she gone?? I missed her so much. In my emotional state, I felt a hand on my shoulder, and I heard a gentle male voice, "Don't worry, Diana, she is with me. I will look after her." And as I turned around I saw my grandfather smile at me and give me another gentle pat on my shoulder. I could let go now as I had always trusted my grandfather - his wisdom and his ways. I knew my mother was in a safe harbor and had found peace with her family of angels in Heaven.

Compassionate Teachers

In 1985 I was the principal of an alternative high school for school dropouts. My school started from a grant given at a time when the dropout rate in the Renton School District was twenty percent. My first task was to hire five teachers for the new school. My second task was to reach out into the community and high schools to recruit students into our program. The school was called The Re Entry Program instead of the words high school which our students already associated with failure. We were located on a Vocational Technical campus so students could learn job skills and a diploma. The school was extremely popular with a waiting list of twenty students.

Interviewing teachers was important to me as I wanted teachers to be compassionate, smart and non-threatening to a fragile population. I also wanted teachers experienced enough not to get fooled by the games dropouts played. I looked for strict teachers with classroom rules who could bend these rules when needed for specific students. Since I built this program from the ground up, I had the latitude of hiring teachers on a six-month probationary period. I could then watch and critique teachers' performance - Could they handle the stress? Could they show compassion when put to the test? Did they know how to individualize the subject matter, tests, and expectations to create success in each student? I ended up with five teachers. Alfreda, Joann, Mark, Tim and Sanford.

Alfreda had high expectations for her students. She was an expert in math and science - all levels. Also, she was young enough to be trained in computer science and kept up with latest electronic technology which was becoming vogue in the 1980's. I thought her classroom rules were too strict and we had numerous conversations about adjusting the rules for the learning or disadvantaged students. I wasn't sure she was a lasting fit for our school. She proved me wrong! Joann had experience with dropouts, had an anti-establishment attitude, had very few rules for her classroom, and loved the students like a mother-hen. She often challenged my rules and became upset with me when a student was dropped from her class. Her specialty was English literature and creative writing.

Her students wrote in daily journals which sometimes created a red-flag situation when she became aware of a student who needed Child Protective Services or suicide prevention. Joann took more sick leave than the rest of the teachers and I suspect she needed the time for her own mental health.

Mark had been a drop-out himself in high school and readily identified with the students. He despised the public school system and was home-schooling his own teenage daughter who later entered the University of Washington in their early entry program for gifted students. Mark was extremely intelligent and gifted in music and art. He looked for success in every student that entered his classroom. His ideas of how to teach were experimental and challenging to his students. He played classical music in the classroom as he believed his students learned better with Strauss and Beethoven in the background. When a new student would enter his classroom, I would often see that student in my office with a scowl on his face. "Do I really have to listen to this classical junk?," he would ask. "Yes," I said, "but give it one week, and if you still don't like Mark's class, I will transfer you to another teacher." In all of the fifteen years Mark worked for me, a student never asked for a transfer.

Tim was the youngest, least experienced teacher who had difficulty with the tough dropouts - the types who had been to jail and wore electronic bracelets on their ankles. He did not like the appearance of some of his students, nor their lack of social habits and often would come complaining to my office. He was an eager learner and was able to adjust his own behavior when I explained his way out of a situation. His background included psychology, science, and math. His psychological skills improved as he learned how not to fall into the traps dropouts used to befuddle and confuse their teachers. He grew to enjoy his students and developed quite a sense of humor over their antics. To this very day he is still teaching dropouts in The Re-entry Program.

Sanford was a black teacher who taught part-time as the only teacher of the evening program that ran from 6:00 to 9:00 pm. He could teach all subjects and liked a relaxed classroom. He was an excellent fit for the night students, who often came tired to class and not always on time. Sanford had few rules but expected the homework to be done. He would let students turn in homework early and leave early. Fifty percent of night students were black, 30 percent Asian, and 20 percent white. Sometimes I would work late to see how the night class was doing and I suspect Sanford told his students I was observing the class so things always looked like everything was on task. I knew this was a tough assignment for any teacher. The evening students were the bread-winners of their families, most of their fathers were absent due to being in prison or being under-employed. Sanford always went to bat for his students, even when I tried to expel a bad apple. Sometimes he won and sometimes I won - but in reality when a drop-out is forced to leave the last chance school, no one wins!

The Converse Box

My pale green eyes are starring straight ahead. I cannot see because I am dead, but I feel as though I am on a joumey through time. Pete and Diana are sitting in the front seat being quieter than normal - probably in an attempt to keep their mixed emotions in check. Their sadness and relief are seesawing through their brains. My owner, Sharon, has my still warm body snuggled in her lap, wrapped tightly in a dark brown towel. She still loves me, even through death. My body died before my brain, which is also common in humans.

My name is Sunflower and I am 18 years old or perhaps I should say 18 years dead. My beautiful orange tabby fur grew tattered and saggy the last six months. I could no longer jump to the bed to sleep with my owner at night, so Sharon would gently lift me up at bedtime and carefully place me on the floor in the morning. I slept on a towel because my bowels were not predictable. Finally, after losing too much weight and having no appetite even for my Frisky treats, Sharon started to realize it was time to help me pass to the other world. This was a hard decision for her to make so she asked her sister, Susan, "Do you think I should put Sunflower to sleep?" "Yes, I do," was her answer. She asked her parents. "Yes, we do," they said. "And we will be there at the vet's office with you so you will not have to do this alone.

Sharon picks a date on her calendar, July 5, and calls her vet to make this fatal appointment. I am a smart, orange, tabby male cat and knew right away that something was going to happen, so I perked up and behaved in a peppy way to let everyone know that I was still okay. But I didn't fool anyone, because I could no longer eat and three days had passed since I had eaten normal food with my cat companions, Lioness and Krammer. The Fourth of July arrives and everyone leaves for the fireworks show in downtown Cle Elum, across the railroad tracks. Sharon tells her parents and friends that she will always remember me on July 4th - an Independence Day for an independent cat.

On Thursday morning, the 5th, I awake early and find myself all curled up in The Converse Box. Little did I know that I would be buried in that same box later in the day. But I knew something was up because Sharon was sitting in her chair, crying with unhappy noises. I try to cheer her up by rubbing against the bottom of her jeans but she will have no part of that - she just sobs louder. Diana, her mother, is also there and starts making trips up and down the stairs with Sharon's backpack, suitcase and a dark brown towel and The Converse Box.

At the vet's office, everyone looks sad - even the people in the white coats. Pete and Diana completely fall apart; tears are sliding down their cheeks. Sharon, looking at her supposedly support group, gathers me up in her arms and takes me into the next room to place me on the table. Later she would laugh and scold her parents for being such wimps in the vet's waiting room. Sharon courageously lays me on the table, all by herself, and holds me while the vet gives me a shot. Next I feel the movement of a vehicle heading west on the highway.

As I sit on Sharon's lap, inside the dark brown towel, I hear Sharon ask, "How much further until we get to LaConner?" Her Dad replies, "About two more hours." "I will take a nap on the back seat with Sunflower, "she says, and snuggles the limp towel tightly to her chest. Later, upon arriving to Pete and Diana's house in Shelter Bay, I feel my owner stir and an argument begins about the size of The Converse Box. Diana thinks it should be a bigger box but Sharon says that Sunflower wants to be buried in the box she brought. The tired mother agrees.

Very quickly after our arrival, I hear the clink of a shovel, then I hear two shovels. Sharon and Pete are father-daughter bonding as if a single motion were taking place. Diana stays inside listening to the silence of the contented pair. Decisions are being made as to the perfect burial spot, the depth, the placement of the Mexican clay sunflower to mark the grave. Finally The Converse Box is lowered down and two shovels are throwing dirt. Sharon asks her Mom to come outside for the prayer. Three adults gather hands and say grateful things about my companionship to Sharon through 18 years.As the letting go takes place, I feel very peaceful and hear the calling of the other animals. I am starting a new life in a new world. Later that day, Sharon looks out to my backyard spot, next to the raspberry and blue berry bushes. Many times the rest of the day she is looking out to the backyard for what she calls a sign. About four o'clock Sharon runs to get her parents, "Come quick," she says. A lone deer stands behind the fence with a head bowed to the exact spot where Sunflower is buried. Large doleful eyes are giving an all knowing look. Sharon smiles and gleefully says, "I knew there would be a sign." The journey is now complete.

Cops and Robbers

The three of us, Pam, Diana and Peter, arrive in Belize City on a Sunday afternoon in 1990 to tropical air and sweet smelling rain forests. Belize City is a small fishing village, the capital of the country Belize, a third world economy located beneath Mexico. After stowing our gear at our waterfront hotel, we set off to explore on foot the neighborhood and find a seafood restaurant for a real dinner, a welcome change from our airplane meals. On our walk we encounter happy children playing in the streets and adults willing to part with homemade crafts for our cash. On our walk downtown we see much evidence of idleness, shacks and hovels, and trashed neighborhoods full of poverty and gang graffiti. But the beautiful wide-eyed, dark haired children smiled and waved at us and we felt truly welcomed in this rainforest paradise.

We are accomplished travelers in third world countries: we leave our jewels at home, dress "down" in jeans, sandals, and old shirts and wear "fanny packs" to hide our cash and credit cards. Our passports and airline tickets are locked in the hotel safe. Looking like the natives usually works for us but not on this particular day.

After a satisfying dinner of fresh fish, we set off on foot to the famous swinging bridge on Belize Canal. This popular tourist stop is full of crowds watching the fishing boats, laden with their daily catch of fresh fish. As the boats approach the bridge two men push the turnstile wheel which opens to let the boats glide through the canal in search of the safety of the local marinas. After dusk the bridge is closed and the crowd disperses.

The darkness is creeping upon us, so we head leisurely to our hotel which is only four blocks away. Two teenagers whiz by on bicycles and I am immediately on alert as I recognize the gang clothing- the black hoods and dropped, baggy jeans. My occupation in Seattle includes the supervision of teenagers, including the local juveniles and gang " wantabees" and my instincts tell me we are in for trouble. Very quickly the kids circle back and stop in front of us. "Give us your stuff," says the kid on our backside. The one in front with the black hood drawn down so far that we can not see his face, draws a gun, which is pointed directly at us. My sister Pam, who tends to giggle in tense situations, looks at me and starts to laugh. I give her my "this is not funny" look and she shuts up. We raise our hands and part with our fanny packs. Another bicycle is coming our way but this is a "friendly", a Japanese dispatcher from a local embassy. He assesses the situation, yells at the kids, and they quickly rush away, with me yelling, "I just want my glasses back."

Later we debrief at our hotel, trying to decide what to do next. We call the states to cancel our stolen credit cards. Our prescription sunglasses will never be recovered but I console myself by thinking that perhaps our glasses will be purchased later by the needy at Black Market value. Our tourist pride has been hurt more than our pocketbooks so we feel lucky. We realize the next action on our part is to notify the local police about the robbery.

At eight o'clock, the unmarked police car pulls up in front of our hotel and wisks us quickly away to the police building. The building seems strange to us, because it is like a fort surrounded by high wire fences and a locked guarded gate. Once inside we follow the officer into the front office and fill out the papers that describe the robbery. We do not look at mug shots because we did not see their faces. The officer wants to take us on a ride through the local neighborhood to see if he can spot the kids he suspects to be the robbers. As we leave the station, he reaches into a drawer and grabs a gun which looks like a beretta, and slips it into his belt. Now we all get back into the unmarked car and off we speed to the local neighborhood gangster hovels to take a look.

I have a bad feeling about this. My sister Pam's body language says it all - her eyes are frozen poached eggs, her face white, and her lips a thin hard line. I know what she is thinking. "We are going to die. Mr. supposedly policeman is taking us down a back alley to shoot us and the gang kids will help him dispose of our bodies." Pam is very quiet but I feel her adrenaline. Peter, on the other hand, is politely chatting up the officer with the usual nice ities about weather, golf, and other stupid stuff. When I am scared, I, unlike my sister, become quite gregarious, so I asked the officer about the gang problem in Belize. He said they indeed had a major problem but were trying to rehab as many teens as they could help. He told us how hard their lives were with parents unemployed, no welfare checks, and a lack of medical and educational services. I explained to him that I well understood the problem, because I was involved in the rescue of gang kids at my Alternative High School in Seattle. I seemed to strike up a common bond with him as we searched the neighborhood, looking for the teen robbers. The dark alleys and poverty-stricken neighborhoods were sad to see and our small robbery seemed unimportant. "Will you be pressing charges against these kids if I locate them, he asked. All three of us said in unison, "NO."

We were so relieved to be dropped back at our hotel. We thanked the officer for his concern. Once in our rooms, we hugged each other, feeling that we had dodged another bullet literally. We had two scary encounters in one day, but couldn't decide which one was the worst - the cops or the robbers.

My Cousin Carole

My cousin Carole and I were close friends growing up together in Northern Minnesota. Carole was born in 1940, the oldest and only child of Aunt Flora and Uncle Frank Rukavina. Two years later I was born in 1942, the oldest child of six children born to Lola and Lester Blume. My house was a noisy unpredictable environment with babies and toddlers on the loose; Carole's home was quiet, organized and predictable with Aunt Flora ever the in charge mother. At the family gatherings, especially the holidays, Carole and I were sidekicks with similar interests. We loved to explore Grandma's attic in the old stucco Victorian home, dancing around to the Victrola music, bicycling around the nearby college campus, and playing dress-ups with Grandma's old furs, laces, and shiny gowns. We would giggle and laugh and try to escape whenever we could to avoid taking care of the younger cousins.

In 1946, Carole had her first seizure. Not much was known about seizures in the 1940's, but Aunt Flora took Carole to all the renown doctors to find a cure, even to the famous Mayo Clinic. My mother took her children aside one day and explained that Carole had seizures and if this happened during our playtime, we should find an adult immediately. Suddenly I felt like Carole's big sister rather than her younger cousin. The word "seizure" scared me. Also, Carole was on a medication that made her somewhat "loopy." But Carole was still my best playfriend and we continued to explore growing up together and sneaking off to the outdoors to escape the relatives. Playing in the snow, ice skating and sledding were popular in Northern Minnesota and we were good at all three.

In 1950, my family moved to Baudette, Minnesota where my Dad took his first teaching job. Carole's father became a high school principal in Birch Bay, Michigan so we were only a few hours away from each other but didn't connect as often after that except at Thanksgiving or Christmas. So Carole and I wrote letters back and forth to fill the gap, which was a popular means of correspondence in the 1950's. I noticed that Carole's letters became difficult to read as her writing skills were on a much lower level than mine. I asked my Mom what was happening to Carole and she said that Carole had had more seizures and the last seizure had caused damage to her brain. This made me feel very sad, like losing a part of myself. Later I learned about the "R" word as the adults talked about Carole's retardation. By now I was in high school and caught up in the "I" world of the teenager. While I was excelling in honor roll classes my cousin Carole was struggling to finish basic language skills on a third grade level. We grew apart intellectually but emotionally we were as strong as ever and continued our friendship and correspondence.

Shortly after high school, I married my high school sweetheart, Peter, and Carole also married her high school sweetheart, Mark Tierney. She had met Mark in her Special Education Program and fell in love much to the dismay of her mother and father, who planned to keep Carole at home with them forever. Mark had an average intelligence in a cerebral-palsy body. Because they did not have the approval of either family, they eloped. The parents of

Carole and Mark had a joint meeting to decide what to do next as both Carole and Mark were age 19 and 20 and had some legal rights of their own. Instead of annulment, both parents decided to let them have a try at being married, since they seemed compatible and in love. Carole was an overweight, loving teddy-bear, who liked to give Mark backrubs, and Mark was very protective of Carole and handled the brainwork of planning and finances. Today, in 2005, Carole and Mark Tierney are still married and live in their own home in Superior, Wisconsin.

Through the years, Pete and I have traveled to Superior to stay with Carole and Mark and check on how they are doing. Carole always greets me with a huge bear hug, always stronger than I would like. Mark has gotten to know us and now trusts us as friends, but lets us know that he is in charge and everything to do with Carole has to come through him. To Carole each day is a new experience and start's with a question, "What is the plan for today?"

She has no yesterdays or tomorrows, just the day she is in and I often think this is more of a blessing than a curse. In Superior, Wisconsin, Carole and Mark are strong members of their local Catholic church, both of them do custodial work for the church and local high school. At four a.m. each day they deliver the Duluth Daily Newspaper to about 200 homes. They have been given awards for their service to the community and are truly loved by many people in this small town that has adopted them.

I will always feel proud of my cousin Carole and what she has done with her life. We still write letters back and forth and talk on the phone. I am her only living relative as both her parents passed away in the 1980's. If her husband, Mark, passes away before she does, I will get the phone call and then will need to decide what the next step will be for Carole, as she will be unable to live by herself. With God's help, I will take care of her no matter what the future brings.

Culture Shock

Finally I had secured my first teaching position. After graduating from Seattle Pacific University at age 33, I was eager and willing to make a difference in the lives of teenagers. Why did it take me so long, you ask? Because I had been a busy stay at home mother of two little girls for seven years. But, when my children went off to school, I became restless to do something different so I decided to explore becoming a teacher and finish up my college education which I had abandoned after my first pregnancy. But now I had that golden teaching certificate and was eager to save the world.

Teaching jobs were hard to come by in 1975, because high school enrollment was dropping and teachers were being laid off according to seniority. The competition was fierce and with no experience, being a mother of two, and wearing a label called "displaced homemaker," I had some twenty unsuccessful interviews before finding my first job. But this job was a guaranteed one year contract with the Seattle School District. The interview had taken place at the downtown Administrative Building so I had not seen the classroom, school building, or the students. This was my FIRST MISTAKE. My SECOND MISTAKE was showing up for my first day with students at Cleveland High School. Somehow my classroom was neither what I had envisioned nor what I had been taught to expect from my internship and educational theory at the university. I was more than a duck out of water. I was about to enter a world of cultural shock and was very ill prepared.

When I arrived at Cleveland High School, I parked my car in a lot that said "park at your own risk." After reporting in to the principal, I was given a brief description of the remedial English class I was teaching and was given the keys to the portable located off site on the backside of the main building. I had started to feel suspicious of my situation and feeling that maybe the job interview had left out some important details. RULE NUMBER ONE: Never sign a teaching contract at an Administration Building without first visiting the high school and talking with the teachers in the building about the job description, but too late for me, of course, because I had already signed a legal one year contract. As I approached the portable, I noticed how stone quiet it was and thought to myself, things aren't so bad after all, I probably had great kids and a lovely classroom. RULE NUMBER TWO: Always be prepared for the worst when you enter a classroom for the first time with high school students.

As I opened my classroom door, I saw some 35 teens reading their books quietly - too quiet was the clue. At my desk sat Lenny, their ringleader, with feet outstretched on the top of my desk, giving the impression that he was also studious. As I walked toward the blackboard, the hair on the back of my neck started to rise and joy was replaced by fear. (Please note here that I had developed alligator skin over the years due to being the oldest of six children and I knew how to not show fear.) My adrenaline rush took over and I calmly, calmly, erased the blackboard where the greeting said, "Welcome to the White Bitch!" Then I wrote in large letters the word RESPECT - FOR TEACHER, CLASSMATES, AND SELF. Being the actor that I was in front of my students, I explained how happy I was to be at their school and was looking forward to helping them learn the important things of life - how to write checks, balance a checkbook, and read excellent literature such as The Blackboard Jungle. Indeed, I was in the Blackboard Jungle - my class was 50 percent Black, 40 percent Asian, and 10 percent White. I instantly knew that I had more to learn from my students than they did from me.

Yes, I did survive my first year of teaching, but I did not do this alone. At the end of my first day I had a meeting with the Vice Principle, Mr. Ed, an Asian man who "spoke softly but carried a big stick." The story was that this particular class had been through four substitute teachers since the beginning of the school year. All substitutes had left over various incidents. So I told Mr. Ed that I had a plan but I would need his help. The next day Mr. Ed followed me to the classroom and I immediately started "throwing" the meanest kids out of my classroom. Lenny was the first to go, Pam the second, and Melee the third. Then I confronted the rest of the class and explained that I knew that no-one had taught them anything for the last two months and that I planned to leave on Friday, since I doubted they really wanted to learn anything and would continue to be uncooperative students. The deal was this: We would have a classroom vote on Friday as to whether Mrs. Caple would stay or not. If you don't want me here, I'm out of here and you can have substitute number six. So, it's up to you!

Tuesday through Thursday I threw all the good stuff I could come up with that would attract the learning styles of these tough

Rainier Beach kids. Every day the students took turns writing on the blackboard what subjects they wished to learn about. I brought in teenage literary books and lots of fresh new magazines like Motor Trend, Seventeen, Hot Rod, and Readers' Digest. By Friday they were beginning to show an interest in learning and I had them hooked. They voted YES on Friday and I stayed and I stayed and I had the most memorable teaching experience of my whole life. The most valuable lesson for me was the feeling of what it was like to be the minority in another culture. No-one could tell you what that was like, nor could I put this into words. I always knew I was a visitor to their cultural world and would never belong. But I also knew I had something they wanted. I could teach them new things and underneath it all they really wanted to learn. Education was a way to escape from some of their daily hardships. I came face to face with teen parenting, drug dealing, gang violence, school lockdowns, and extreme poverty. But in the end, we developed a mutual respect society, where learning could take place.

The Depth of Vision

I never really saw the world until I was 56 years old. Sure, I had traveled the world, studied human behavior, taught high school students for 20 years. Visually speaking, I had never really explored the objects in front of my eyes. When I left my work world at age 56, I was hungry for new beginnings, new hobbies, new friends. I needed to experiment with my own ideas and discover the new me - whoever she might be. Peter and I became snowbirds and settled in Tucson, Arizona to explore the desert and mountains surrounding us. Having done this for a year, I still felt unsettled and somewhat bored. I missed my work world, my educational friends, and had literally no challenge in my life.

My challenge came in the disguise of a friendship as I met a real artist on one of my hikes. Geri Niedermiller talked me into joining an art class with her while the two husbands went golfing.

I knew this to be totally out of my element so I said, "Yes, I'll give it a try." She dragged me to the nearest art store, where we bought a hundred dollars worth of art supplies - all quality stuff, like high textured white drawing pads (acid free), colored pencils known as prismacolor, artist's erasers used for blending and mixing color, etc. etc. The headache in the back of my brain was saying "just because you have a hundred dollars worth of fishing gear, does not mean you can fish or even catch a fish."

Geri picked me up at my apartment the first day and off we went with our professional looking black artist's suitcases, neatly organized inside with enough stuff to last five years. On this very first day of putting my toe into the water, I almost bolted out of shear fright. I was the only beginner in the room. The other artists were so polished as to have their own art shows at the downtown galleries. I could quickly tell that Geri knew what she was doing and her modest remarks about her talent were lost in the pencil movements of her first drawing in class. I was not only over my head, I didn't even know the basics. "Oh, well, hang in there, girl. " These artist types seem glad to have you and said the usual encouraging words that they were beginners at one time too. This was little consolation to me, as I was the only beginner in the room. I did no drawing that first day but walked around the room as an observer. Each artist explained to me what drawing goal they were working on and described various techniques used to produce shadows, textures, three dimensional depths, etc. This fifteen person group had been drawing together for many years, traveling to workshops together, and basically had advanced their drawing techniques from spending six hours a week producing quality art in a workshop room at the Tucson Elk's Club. By the end of my first day, I knew where to start and that's really all I needed to do was have a place to start, so I returned to the art store and bought basic drawing books and next week I started on shading techniques for shadows.

I spent seven .years with this artist's group and still today dearly love each and everyone of them. We listened to classical music and visited with one another as we drew our masterpieces. All talk was encouraging and when we discovered a new way to create a texture, a new blend of color, or another way to observe the same flower or bird; we shared our ideas. I started the class a beginner and I left the class a beginner, but my observation skills of what I see around me changed dramatically. To draw an object or a person is to truly see - the vision of the details is so different than the first glance. My mentor became Ann Kullberg who is a nationally recognized prismacolor portrait artist. I attended every workshop of hers that I could find and learned the step by step process of visualization and imitation. My eyes had been missing so much of the world - now I can stop, slow down and truly drink in the details of what I look at. The depth of this looking is never ending and I can return again and again to the same object and see another perspective. I have learned to draw upside down and sideways. Now, I am age 65, and I am still enjoying the depth of vision with my grandchildren who instantly see the details - and the touch, the smell, the pulling apart, the putting together of their immediate environment. "What do you see," I ask as I hold Sam or Devon up to the window.

Diving in Belize

"What would you like to do? my sister asks me with a look that says she already knows what she would like to do. Sisters often read each other's minds and I knew what she was thinking. "Let's go snorkeling again on the coral reefs. It's such a calm sunny day. We can bring our underwater cameras and take more pictures of the sea creatures," I replied.

Husband Peter was gone for the day on a scuba diving trip with eight other tourists. The dive vessel, fifty feet long, diesel engines, had a captain and two crew members. The country of Belize is noted for the best dives in the world and he was excited to explore the waters off the coast of San Pedro. Pam and I were also happy to have a girls' day and were soon off on a power boat headed towards the barrier reefs off San Pedro, second in beauty to the famous barrier reefs in Australia. The skipper of the powerboat dropped us off at the usual spot and then tied his boat to one of the buoys allowed for tourist boats only. A one mile square of barrier reef was allowed for tourist exploration, leaving eighty percent of the reef natural and untouched by contaminating tourists. San Pedro Island was mostly undeveloped in the early 1990's. We had arrived to the island via a small bush plane, a six-seater. No cars were allowed on the island but golf carts and donkeys were common transportation. The main industry was lobster fishing so the island was surrounded by docks, fishing vessels, and a large breakwater that opened in the middle to allow the lobster boats in and out of the harbor.

Pam popped her head out of the water and said, "Did you see the school of seahorses?" "Yes, "I replied, but they were in front of my face so close that I couldn't take a picture - seems they enjoyed looking me over, too." My camera was loaded with film and I submerged to gaze at the wonders of color - stripped red and black, stripped yellow and turquoise, grey slippery needlefish, and much more. Click, click went my camera. I took pictures of my sister underwater too. We had paid for two hours of snorkeling so soon the power boat came to pick us up. Once ashore, we walked back to our hotel room at the Belize Yacht Club.

After hot showers we headed to town for some serious shopping, to buy colorful matching shorts and tops in tropical prints. Prices were cheap and we loaded up on clothing and beach towels. The stores were rustic with sand floors. Bartering was the popular way to get a deal, so we pooled our items for even lower prices.

After a lobster lunch we spent the afternoon napping and reading our novels. No television or electronics on this island. We were lucky to have one telephone at our hotel. The bang-pop of a thunderstorm awoke us. We looked outside to the blackest sky we had ever seen. Pam and I looked at each other with serious faces. Peter's dive vessel was not due back until four o'clock. He was still a long way from port. We tried to concentrate on our reading, but soon I said, "I'm going down to the dock to talk to the dock master. He had a ship to shore radio and tracked the vessels out in the open seas. "Yes, he said," I have sent messages to all the dive boats to seek shelter as a gale force storm is brewing. We are expecting winds up to sixty miles per hour." I returned to the hotel, trying to read, but praying for a safe return for my beloved Peter. The waiting time was horrifically unpleasant. My stomach sat in the middle of my throat and my eyes were watery. Four o'clock came and went.

"Pam, I'm going back down to the dock." By now the skies were inky black, visibility nil, and the force of the wind barely kept me upright. I wore my life-jacket in case the wind knocked me off the dock. I managed to slide one foot at a time forward until I reached the dock master who was extremely busy with the radio.· He recognized me and said the most awful news ever, "Sorry mamm, but we lost radio contact with the dive vessel a half hour ago." My heart took a lurch. "However, he continued, "we have survival boats going out to the breakwater opening to shoot off flares so, hopefully, they will find their way into the harbor." Hanging on to the sides of the dock and inching my way back to safety, I knew I could only wait and pray. By six o'clock I was thinking the worst. Pam's demeanor was as frightened as mine. No longer able to read, we sat in stony silence and listened to rain pounding on the windows with a force so heavy we moved away from the windows into the center of the room. The waiting was the worst part for me, but I dare not go out into the winds. San Pedro had few outdoor lights and the evening darkness had caused an almost zero visibility. I could only imagine what was happening outside the harbor in the fifteen foot seas. The winds had reached sixty miles per hour. The palm trees were dancing close to the ground. The occasional snap of a branch could be heard.

"Pam, I can't stand this waiting, I'm going down to the dock. At least we can listen to the radio with the dock master." By six thirty a group of relatives and friends of the divers had gathered by the dock master's shack. People whispered and held hands. The bright red flares lit up the black sky. The only boat yet to return was Peter's dive vessel. Finally a weary battered vessel appeared a few feet away. We were all eager to help with the lines and grab the clumsy tourists as their sea-legs where unsteady on the ground. Peter's face was an ashen grey and we knew he been terribly frightened. The gear on the boat had been smashed and damaged but no one cared about the gear. Pam and I helped carry Peter off the dock, as he wobbled sideways and blindly stumbled up and down.

So gleefully grateful of the outcome, Pam, Peter, and I were soon discussing where to go for dinner. Peter said, "Only soup for me, my stomach is still out to sea." At the dinner table, Peter talked and talked about his ordeal. "The first dive, in the morning, the currents under the surface were so strong that I got sick with my dive mask on," But I remembered what my son-in-law Christopher said and blew outward to clear my mask. We did see the most amazing things underwater at about 80 feet below. A row of large lobsters swam by like railroad cars so close to each other they may have been connected. Colorful tropical fish, orange and yellow coral, sea turtles were hard to see because of the murky water. The master diver cancelled the second dive due to rough seas. The third dive was a murky dive also but then the storm hit and the radio warned the captain to hurry back. On our way back we were in the eye of the storm and could barely see. The rains were horizontal, the skies black, and the waves at fifteen feet. The radio antenna was torn off the boat by the wind. Like everyone on board, I hung on for dear life."

We wanted to hear more, but our food had arrived. Peter was having lobster soup. Pam and I were having two fresh lobsters apiece. The afternoon waiting and worry had given us voracious appetites. A's we were chowing-down, Pam looked at Peter and said, "What an awful storm. Those seas are probably still rocking and rolling." And she talked she used a hand motion up and down through the air. Peter turned pea green, pushed himself away from his food, and ran for the exit door. Pam and I started uncontrolled laughter as we couldn't help ourselves. Peter never came back to the table.

The Divorce

In 1966 my parents decided to get a divorce. At this time I was already married to Peter and living in Newport, Rhode Island where Pete was stationed in the US Navy. The announcement of their divorce did not surprise me as my parents seemed a mismatched pair while I was growing up. This divorce was the only divorce in the family on both sides, the Blumes and the Cochranes. It was a major event that changed the lives of my parents and all their children.

The 1960s was a confusing time of social changes: women were obtaining equal rights with men, the ugly unpopular war of Viet Nam was on tv every night displaying more and more body bags as the losing war was coming to an end, Nixon had been impeached, and the hippies were rioting in the streets. The women of the 1940s and 50's had been taught to "stifle it!" as Archie Bunker often told Edith on the "All in the Family" tv show. My mother had put up with a lot from my dad during their 23 years of marriage and had finally wanted out- the last straw being his cheating on her while on his very long business trips.

Living on the East Coast had brought me a much needed respite from my parents and siblings. I was now a free agent enjoying making decisions by myself and for myself. Peter had long voyages at sea on the "Charles S. Sperry" destroyer. I worked as a keypunch operator on the Navy base and then later in downtown Providence, R.I. Although I was concerned about my parents' divorce, I felt lucky to be out of the family fray. I was worried about my siblings who were caught up in the fallout of a divorce. My younger sister Pam moved in with dad and lived in Edmonds, while going to a nursing school. My other sister, Flora, and three younger brothers stayed with my mother who moved to the University District to rent a house.

I do not know much about the divorce fallout because I was absent from the whole event. I do know a few things but my memory is hazy about this unpleasantness so I can only speculate and wonder about the entire mess which in those days was a secretive experience. Divorce, like sex and money, were never discussed with the children. When Peter and I got out of the Navy, we rented a house in the Freemont District. This was not too far from mother and my sibs so I could visit occasionally. It was shocking to me to see my mother so badly affected by the divorce. My dad had been responsible for all the financial support and the divorce settlement favored my dad, he ended up with the house, furniture, and of course a steady income. My mother received some child support to help raise the children but it was not enough to sustain the household. She had never worked outside her home and had no work skills. She took a real estate class, got her license, and worked selling homes in the University District. Financial struggle was ever present and I know she had second thoughts about the divorce. But my dad liked his freedom and soon was dating again. My mom asked him if he would like to raise the boys who were now in their teen years and he said, "No, absolutely not!"

My father called me up one day and asked me to come to the house for dinner. He never did this so I was suspicious about his reasons but I showed up for the telltale dinner anyway. After I got to the house, he seemed quite nervous but he had prepared a delicious steak dinner. We sat by the bay window overlooking Puget Sound.We had the usual strained conversation while eating our meal. Later he brought the dessert, a store purchased cherry pie. He wasn't the father I remembered as he fussed over the kitchen work, clearing the table and putting the dishes to soak.I had never seen him do kitchen work before. Also, he was complimenting me on my job and making my marriage work. Sniffing the dubious air in the room, I knew something big was coming. "Well, Diana," dad said, "I am thinking about getting married again." I hadn't expected this and felt like yelling, "I don't really give a Damn!" Instead I listened as he kept on with the conversation. "Her name is Eileen. I think you would like her. She has a college degree and works at the Ballard Hospital as a dietician. She is 13 years younger than me and has never been married. I wanted you to be the first to know. Please tell me how you feel." My dad had never asked me in my whole life how I felt about anything and I felt the old anger flaring up. In a calm voice I replied, "I think the decision should be yours and if you truly wish to be married again than you will have my blessing. But, I will not tell the family about this matter, you will have to do that yourself." "I will, he said. He walked me to my car, we said goodbye, I waved on the way out and wondered how I really felt about all this - another life changing event.

Doctor Frankenstein

The smell was a combination of ether, pickling brine, and rotting flesh. We had been guided into this cold room by Dr. Franklin, known to his students as Dr. Frankenstein. This large anatomy and physiology lab at the University of Washington Medical School contained twenty cadavers. Dr. Franklin was explaining how lucky the first year nursing students were to have a practice lab. Eventually we would be assigned to our very own cadaver, would be given a pass card to the lab, and could come and go as we wished. This was my first day in the lab and my first view of a pickled dead body.

The skin of the gray decaying body had been pulled to the sides to expose a man's large chest cavity, showing areas of black charred lungs due to past smoking habits. Pickled cadavers have shades of light gray, dark gray and black.

Dr. Franklin was using plucking instruments to spread the muscles, arteries and veins into bundles so we could take copious notes, all the time giving the matter medical, scientific names. An image of tossed gray spaghetti noodles came to mind and I felt a lurch in my stomach. I covered my mouth and instantly fell backwards.

Later, I woke up in the hallway on a gurney, still wearing my white lab coat and rubber gloves. Looking around I spied two other students on gurneys. How embarrassing! I was a pretty tough cookie but this lab experience had caused me to faint. Dr. Franklin would probably give me an "F" for the day. He was a hard hearted unfriendly man who disliked teaching. Rumor had it that Dr. Franklin had done much-needed grant writing and research for the U of W in his younger days. Now he was old and useless, so the university kept him on as a nursing instructor so he could continue his tenure. Students kept their distance from him as he was grouchy and smelled bad like stale whisky. His pocked wrinkled face always had a frown, a red clown nose looked misplaced, and his white lab coat had stains and needed bleach. Actually, Dr. Frankenstein's whole body needed bleach!

Standing at the podium in the lecture hall, Dr. Franklin's first day speech had said it all. "Look around you. One half of you, 50%, will not be here at the end of this quarter. Nursing is not for the faint of heart. Learning the anatomy and physiology of a human being is essential to your training. The body is a work of science. Each muscle has a purpose. Each artery has a purpose.Each organ has a purpose. As you learn the correct medical definitions and study these various parts, you will gain an appreciation for the inter-connectedness of the mechanics of the body. I expect you to study each day. Always be prepared for the "pop" quiz. Each week's knowledge builds on the previous week's knowledge. Those of you who keep up with me will make it and those who don't will not make it."

I never forgot this speech by a teacher who was out to get me instead of helping me learn. To continue on into nursing, one had to pass his class. But, here I was lying in the hallway on a gurney, having fainted in the lab. This was the beginning of inner doubts. Maybe I shouldn't become a nurse after all. I had pulled average grades my first year at U of W but still felt unhappy in such a large impersonal environment - a small-town girl who felt lost at sea. I really had no idea what I wanted for a career. I had a steady boyfriend and most of my girlfriends were married with babies. Fainting in the medical lab had put me at the crossroads. I felt a pressure to run away.

However, I did return to my cadaver who I eventually called "Jake." I learned more about human anatomy than I ever wanted to know but it was not enough for Dr. Franklin. I flunked the final exam. Only 50% of his class passed just as he had predicted. The "flunkeys" were told to repeat the class next quarter or chose another major. I did neither; I dropped out and got married.

Do Unto Others

The oldest child in a family of eight, I was care-taking at age four for Sister Baby Pam. After the rest of the brood came along, Flora, Mark, Lester, and Herman, I had mastered the art of being the second mother in the family. "To be or not to be a care-taker" does not exist in my highly efficient organized brain. I was born a care taker and still to this day love helping others. "Diana will do it," my parents said everyday and now "Diana will do it!" is as natural to me as taking my next breath.

Growing up as my mother's right hand, I was recognized in my neighborhood as the most responsible teen for babysitting. My Dad's doctor clients were always calling for me to sit their children, sometimes even into the wee hours of the night as they delivered babies at the local hospital or simply stayed out late to dance and party. In my family, my aunts always talked about how I would gather all the children into a playroom and organize games for them, including sometimes 15 children at a time. I think I loved all my wee relatives but I also loved the power and recognition. I knew early in life that care-taking was my destiny and at college I majored in Social Science and Special Education and loved the challenge of working with difficult people.

My educational teaching years were an extension of my growing up in a big family. I loved being the master of my classroom and helping children grow, fostering their learning gifts, and helping with the social transitions of life. When I retired I thought I would make a marvelous substitute teacher, until I realized that I could not bond with students in that role. The $25 a day combat pay certainly was not worth it. When my husband, Pete, retired in 1993, we moved to LaConner into grandma's house on Elwha Drive. I looked around my new neighborhood with pleasure. What a perfect place for a care-taker to live. Most of my neighbors were elderly and still are, so perhaps I could be of some service to this community. My brain is thinking, "Diana will do it!"

Needing something useful to do, I saw an advertisement in the Skagit Valley Herald for a hospice class in Sedro Wooley. I had stayed with my mother during her hospice care at Tucson Medical Center and found the dying and death experience to be something I could handle. Indeed all my brave brothers and sisters left me holding the bag during my mother's final hours. "Diana will do it," they said as they headed for their hotels. Call us when it's over. So I did.

As brave as I am, I had some reservations about the hospice class, but reminded myself it was just a class, and I didn't have to do anything I didn't want to - one of the great advantages of being retired. Ha! So off I went, notebook in hand, for another adventure. Not only did I enjoy the six week class but I have learned to be even calmer in a crisis situation of illness, death, and dying. Another benefit of the class is learning all the resources available in Skagit Valley - ministers, support groups, funeral homes, prayer groups, etc. My husband Peter has joined me in being a hospice helper for our neighborhood. When an ambulance arrives at a neighbor's house, Pete and I are quickly on the scene to give emotional support to the neighbor who often is alone during the crisis while waiting for a family member to arrive. Mostly it's just a matter of being an extra set of eyes and ears and adding a familiar trusting face to the group of strangers who arrive on the scene to administer life saving skills.

However, sometimes we do much more. Each ambulance arrives to a new situation and we learn more each time we show up. Sometimes we drive the spouse to the hospital and stay with him or her while the minister or doctor gives the death news. Sometimes we help scatter ashes, sometimes we go to the funeral home as extra eyes and ears while the left-behind person makes the necessary burial arrangements. Through hospice we have learned there is no right or wrong as to how people handle death. Each person copes in his or her own way. But I am grateful to God for giving me the care-taking skills that have followed me through my life from the oldest child in a family of eight, to a vocation in teaching, and now as hospice helper to my neighbors. Diana will do it and still does!

Emily's Victory

As I arrived at the Saratori School in the Renton neighborhood I saw Emily's car parked at the curb. Seven o'clock a.m. was an unusual time for a teenager to visit me but was a normal time for me to start my workday. I wore several hats on my job - high school principal, counselor, building manager, and crisis trouble shooter for teen parenting, drug abuse, gang wantabees, etc. Emily looked needy as she slumped behind her wheel, like maybe she had slept there all night. But I had startup things to do before I could deal with Emily.

First I unlocked the main building door and turned off the alarm system. Next I activated the video cameras, listened to any emergency messages I might have on my recorder. Dealing with the teen age emergencies of the day was a large part of my job, but hearing nothing life threatening, I continued down the hall to open all the classrooms for the teachers who would be arriving at 7:30 a.m. Our alternative school was a last chance opportunity for the dropouts from the local high schools. We served 150 students in six classrooms and taught individualized curriculum, which included remediation, gifted, and special education depending on the needs of each student. The dropout population included many "loner" type kids who even at age 16 were taking care of themselves while living in dysfunctional households or in an apartment on their own. Emily was age 17, had grown up in foster homes, but now had received an emancipation verdict from the court so she was legally responsible for herself. Although only 17 she tended to hang around with the twenty year old crowd. She loved going to our school and was a favorite student with much potential and intelligence.

My secretary, Judy, soon arrived and said, "You better see Emily right away, before school starts and she shoved a sorry looking Emily into my office and closed the door." Judy had a knack for prioritizing the teen age emergencies. I had been busy at my desk and when I looked up I almost cried. It was obvious that Emily had been badly battered and bruised. Her face looked like the dark spots on a banana, her eyes were swollen from her tears, and her neck had dark red and blue rings on it as though she had been strangled. I was an experienced CPS counselor and knew the stages of domestic violence. I knew this was a brave step Emily had made to show up at my office. Calmly I sat back and asked Emily to tell me her story. I listened and listened and listened. Finally she had cried herself out and said she didn't know what to do as she loved her boyfriend so much and this was the first time he had gotten violent with her. (Rule No. 1 - Do not believe the victim and the cover-up stories they love to tell.) The violence had taken place at the University of Washington dorm, in the boyfriend's room where Emily had decided to stay the night. He was 23 years old. I told Emily that I had to fallow the legal procedure which meant a CPS report to my school district and a phone call to the police. She protested of course, but a part of her trusted me and she was in a lot of physical pain. I took a hard line approach as I was trained to do and asked her if she wanted to be responsible for the death of another young girl. "If you do not report this to the police and press assault charges, the next victim will not be this lucky, I said." Not concerned so much about herself, she was frightened that another person might get hurt. She agreed to go with the police officer who had arrived and also to press charges against the University of Washington student. After her statement was taken by the police and pictures of her face and neck were taken, she was treated at the nearby Valley General Hospital and sent home.

It was hard for Emily to return to her normal life of work and school, but her support system at school included several teachers and students who were sympathetic to her story. Two months later I received a subpoena at my office to report to the downtown Seattle court building to testify on Emily's behalf. When I arrived at the courthouse, I met Emily and her court appointed lawyer. The U of W student was pleading "not guilty" and had hoped to get off. As we sat in the courtroom I saw the young man in a smartly fashioned suit, sitting next to not one, but three, well dressed lawyers from the University of Washington's legal department. I knew Emily was getting cold feet but I had enough anger if or the two of us and was determined to see justice done. Of course, when the case came to the judge's attention, he looked at his calendar and delayed the trial for two weeks. This delay tactic took place three times and each time required an absence from my building of four hours and the coordination of the witnesses. I do think that the delays work in the favor of the guilty as some witnesses get tired of the subpoenas and discussed with the slowness of the legal process and simply don't show up. Finally, after the fourth subpoena, the lawyers had a meeting and settled out of court. Rob, the U of W student, changed his plea to "guilty", was given six months in jail and most importantly was given a criminal record of assault. This was Emily's moment to shine; she had persevered and received the justice she deserved. I could only hope she would choose her next boyfriend more carefully.

My Emotional Stretch

The most intimate journey my brain can visit is the deep crevices of my emotions. No conversation with another human has taken me to such depths. I became attached to this experience at a very early age as I discovered a creative way to relieve high anxiety and express myself. As a victim of the child rearing days of the 1940's, I was often told to sit down and be quiet. This behavior was unacceptable to my bright, curious, assertive imagination so paper and pen became my comfortable escape. And, I will be escaping into this format for the rest of my life.

At age 65, I still find the mysteries of written exploration an exciting place to go. My writing group of like-minded souls are fun to be with once a week at the Senior Center at Maple Hall. Our teacher, Claire Swedberg, is a talented journalist who is not afraid to joggle our writing brains with new ideas each week. We create a new story or poem once a week, agonize over the process of editing, and finally read our masterpieces to the critical ears of our accomplished peers. Many people would flee from such a task but we willing show up for more punishment each week and the gift we receive is the opportunity to process our writings from mere beginnings to metaphors, similes and personifications of the nth degree.

Writing for me provides a release of intellectual energy, winding down the various paths of my life into past, present, and future emotions. Perhaps I write my stories because I have an ongoing love affair with pen, paper and computer. Perhaps I was born with a specific DNA gene that restlessly lives inside my brain and constantly cries out - "Today you must write!" Perhaps I feel it is my civic duty to explain every emotion I feel to others so they too will feel this process of being a human being. Paper and pen are still my best friends and also the height of my greatest frustrations. My emotional stretch works well to awaken the paralyzed emotions that most humans are unable to express. I cannot write without compassion even if I annoy myself and others in the process.

Editing is my emotional bane! Rewriting and fixing my stories until they mind me like the spoiled child who won't give up without a fight. Yes, I fight with my writings and my words become alive and demand to be fussed over until perfection of thought and emotion become one. It is hard to confess that I often don't know where my story or poem is going as it often takes on a life of its own and I am treading water to keep up. Words are rushing too fast to put down on paper and I know I must tap into my deep emotional resources to capture the feeling of all that is happening.

My ideas are tumbling forwards and backwards and at the same time sideways - like the cars tumbling down the steep plunge of a roller coaster ride. The feeling of writing sometimes is so intense that at the end of a story, I often feel like I've been on a glorious trip to a white sandy beach - but I don't know how I got there. And, of course, I know this has been a dream and now I must come back to reality. Am I crazy?

I certainly hope so!

Since my writing world is full of ups and downs, cutting and pasting, tears of joy and tears of sorrow, WHY I ask am I so compelled to torture myself. The answer is simply in the one magic sentence that strikes a cord, the perfectionism of word arrangement that reveals the exact thought or idea from writer to reader. Do you understand what I'm trying to say - ???? Yes, I do, smiles the reader. The climax is complete - the emotional connection is worth all the effort.

Female Leadership

In my opinion despite the liberation of women in the 60's, 70's, and 80's, the power of women in the American society is shifting backwards. Women in 2004 live in a male dominated society which still controls the powerful options and decisions of the global markets and political roundtables. There was a glimmer of hope for female power with Madeline Albright, Hillary Clinton, and Martha Stewart. We saw female pilots, female CEO's, female doctors, dentists, engineers, scientists and administrators in the 90' s in America and in many free societies. Now in 2004 we see women hidden behind the veils and men waging war upon other men. The hidden women with no power should be a concern to us all. There by the grace of God go I. I do not want to see a life with less options for women, nor do I wish to see more wars waged by men upon other men.

In my opinion the world will only become a safer place for women and children, when women represent half the government, which means half the Senate and half the House of Representatives.

I really thought back in the 60's and 70's that the shift of power to women from men was starting to happen. Many women working in the 70's and 80's like myself were able to break down the barriers that kept women from achieving equal rights in the work world. We really wanted to create the equal opportunities for our children that we did not have, so that women would be able to climb the corporate and political ladders without hitting the "glass ceilings" or "the good old boys' clubs." In 2004 we have seen the "good old boys' clubs" rise to supreme power in government and corporations. In 2004 women's wages still are 30% less than men's wages.

In my opinion, television depicts females at their worst, still stuck in the "Desperate Housewives" stage in suburbia. All the intelligent female actors on television on the popular shows (doctors, lawyers, airline executives, police women, etc.) still wear little clothing or tight fitting clothes and flirt with all the men on the show. If I had behaved that way when I was an administrator in education, I would have been fired for sexual harassment. Female ladder climbers in the real world are a tough breed and are too busy trying to do it all to have time for sexual pleasures with their male peers. Perhaps I take this view too seriously but I wish for better female roll models for my grandchildren.

In my opinion, illegal immigration is contributing to the decline in female equal rights in this country. The fastest growing illegal immigrations are Hispanic and Middle Eastern. Many times the females in these cultures do not make it to the United States until long after the male is established. Both these cultures encourage women to stay home, have babies, and keep their opinions to themselves. The work world and political offices are for the men only. And when I see the nightly news reports on television, I see lots of stories about violent men (violent stories about war, neighborhood crime, and threatening speeches by men as leaders of their countries). Where have all the women gone?

In my opinion, female leadership has the potential to create a gentler and kinder society; a society where money for bombs and military can be turned into food for starving children. Outsourcing of goods and products can be a goal of equal distribution instead of buying another Lear jet for another wealthy CEO. Mediation between nations can result in peace and prosperity for all, instead of competition to build more nuclear weapons. The truth is all women of all countries want the same for their children - safety, shelter, food, health, and education. If women bring these common bonds to leadership roles, our world will become a safer, peaceful place.

Fiftieth Class Reunion

The fiftieth 1960 class reunion looms ahead-only hours away at the home of Joe McIntosh, old mechanic friend of Pete's. I don't remember him and after 50 years I doubt if he would recognize me either. I am in the bathroom primping like a teenager getting ready for the Senior Prom. A second coat of bright orange polish is applied to my fingers to match the look of my toenails. My hair sports a new look, a side braid, and an inverted short bob. Still I can't hide my face wrinkles and turkey neck. New brown jeans, a beige camisole, and Arizona print complete the look. Pete calls from the West Wing to ask which shirt he should wear with his new blue jeans. We decide on a green and black stripped polo shirt. Feeling like ugly ducklings we hop in the car and head for Lynnwood.

This event is supposed to be a casual picnic outdoors, but we know better. The event is from noon to four on August 31, 2010. Arriving in Lynnwood from our home in LaConner, we stop at the Red Lobster for a gourmet lunch, shrimp fettuccini and halibut wrapped in parchment paper. By one o'clock, our stomachs are satisfied, nerves consoled, and confidence levels return. No picnic food for us and we doubt that many of the 68 year olds will be picnicking either. At a respectable arrival of one-thirty, we park our Acura below the long curving driveway and descend to the house on the hill, pleasantly located in Olympic Estates. We notice the five car garage at the top of the hill and alongside the driveway are several classic cars - 1960 red corvette, 1949 blue ford coupe, 1936 silver delivery-van Plymouth, among several others. Pete immediately heads towards the comfort of the old cars as he loves the old classics.

Wonderful, I'm thinking to myself, Pete will have plenty to talk about so I walk over to the girls' group to see if I can figure out who is who. There seems to be two distinct female groups - the old and decrepit and the surgical repaired.

White and gray hair for the old; the other group brunette, blonde, and henna. Never have I felt so exposed, nor surrounded by so many strangers who are full of smiles and hugs in such an artificial way. Can I go home now, my inner self proclaims. No, Pete and I had agreed to stay a respectable amount of time and be sociable which is not high on our priority list.

I lock on a cheerful smile and turn into a magical social being and start the guessing game. "Marjorie, how good to see you again. Are you still living in Monroe? Mary, how good to see you again. Are you still living in Magnolia? Rosemary, how good to see you again. What a gorgeous outfit you have on, the colors are perfect for the fall. How old are your grandchildren? And, look, there is Roberta, so well preserved, laughing and giggling like a school girl. She has not changed one bit. Beverly, how are you. Did you arrive by plane or do you live in the local area. By now, I am thinking, that I should be expanding on my questions. What else can I say. I need more questions? Never-mind, just keep smiling and listen, let them do the talking.

Wandering through the garage, filled with 1950's antique auto parts and posters, I find plenty more interesting things to do like reading old newspapers and examining antique posters. Joe had not been a scholar in high school but had spent most of his time working at the local auto parts store in Lynnwood which he later purchased as a young man in his 20's. While many of us grads went off to college, Joe and his partner, Dell, established a profitable auto parts business and became well off. High school is certainly not an indicator of people's future careers, but just the beginning. Last week an old boyfriend, Bob, had called me to see if I was coming to the reunion. He told me he had been working on one of the reunion committees, and saw my name and phone number so decided to call. He went on and on about his own life story, becoming an electrical engineer, working for British Petroleum for 25 years, in Alaska on the pipeline. He had been a non-social type in high school who tended to be a loner. In our class yearbook, under his picture, was nothing. We were warming up to each other's voices, when he asked me if I was still married to Pete. He politely said to say hello to Pete. We agreed to meet at the reunion but he never showed.

Ninety minutes later, I find my husband following me around and giving me the let's go stare. Yes, I am ready to go also, so we sneak out of the garage and start down the windy driveway. On our way home we discuss the highlights of this unusual event. "How many people did you recognize," Pete asks. "Ten people out of 150," I reply, and that was a challenge. I kept calling people by the wrong name. Do you think we'll go to the next reunion?" I ask. "Probably, we will," says Pete, "Unless we end up on the deceased list." Thinking about that, I feel content that I was able to visit with a few old classmates.

Fourteen Miles

On September 10th, 1999, we were packed and ready for a first day of cruising to Vancouver, B.C. Our boat, Coralee, had been grounded by Pete's surgeon due to no travel allowed after Pete's endoscopy with Dr. Sible. Several biopsies had been taken and Pete was suppose to rest and stay on a mild diet. The Shelter Bay Yacht Club left without us two days earlier.

September 10th proved to be a warm, sunny day with no fog and flat, calm waters. We had not taken our boat to Vancouver, B.C. before so we were excited about a new cruise. We left early, 6:00 am, and made a full day of cruising with no stops until we got to the Vancouver Yacht Club. On this trip we saw the most orca ever in our eight years out at sea. The orcas were traveling swiftly like porpoises do with much of their sleek black and white bodies out of the water. We traveled with the orcas from Roberts Bay all the way up the Surgeon Bank to the entrance of Vancouver Bay.

After docking, Pete called in our CANPASS number which registered us with the Canadian Customs office. The rest of the day we hobnobbed with our yacht friends, took walks in downtown Vancouver, and later had a gourmet dinner at the Vancouver Yacht Club. We had only missed one docking on this trip so we felt happy to be back in the fold and under the wise care of the yacht skippers.

We slept well that night and looked forward to the "only fourteen miles" crossing in the morning to Bowan Island.

When traveling with our yacht club, different members volunteered as port captains. This meant they were the first to arrive and had planned activities for the group. Activities included potlucks, scavenger hunts, fine dining at a local restaurant, or a visit to a museum or famous landmark. We were told by the port captain that the morning crossing would be easy and we could leave anytime we liked. On September 10th we checked in with the Bowan Island port captain, who had already arrived from an earlier crossing. "Come on over, anytime you like" he had said. "The waters were a bit turbulent with four foot waves but we crossed the fourteen miles just fine. See you when you arrive." I have to explain that when joining a yacht club there are two types of vessels, the sailboats and the power boats. Our port captains had crossed early in the morning in a 30 foot sailboat. Their comments of an "okay" crossing had seemed dubious.

At nine o'clock am we met up with several Shelter Bay boats out in the bay and lined up for the short trip to Bowan Island. We headed out into the strong wind, 30 knots, and had a strong current in our favor pushing us toward Lion gates Bridge. After passing under the bridge, the currents turned on us like an eddy, the wind direction changed, and all of a sudden we were traveling in six foot swells. The current was now against us and we knew we had an unpleasant ride ahead of us, but only for fourteen miles I am thinking to calm my nerves. The situation was much like crossing under Deception Pass during a tide change but in much heavier seas. I sat on the fly bridge with Pete and surveyed the white caps crossing our bow. Although both us had lifejackets on, neither of us wanted to swim in this eddy. Pete looked at my whipped hairdo and white worried face, and said, "It's going to be okay, we can do this." He turned into a large wave and we rode up the wave and then into empty air space as we careened downwards.

The power boat ahead of us had lost an anchor overboard. The wife was at the helm while the skipper was wrestling with the anchor, trying to pull it up onto the boat without falling overboard himself. I am now praying, "Our father who art in Heaven..." I do this when I am nervous and it seems to help. I had been watching the vessel behind us, our dear friends, Frank and Mae, who were copying our technique with the waves but were traveling too close to our stern. I wanted to yell out to them to back up but I knew they wouldn't hear and probably couldn't reverse their boat anyway. Soon I noticed that Mae had gone below. I knew she was spread out on the lower bunk with a bucket in her hand. She gets seasick and overly wrought in rough seas.

I kept my eye on the far waters that seemed to be calmer. I realized that this fourteen miles would take a lot longer than expected as Pete had slowed the boat to eight knots to keep a steady upward flow with a lighter crash landing. We never talked during this time. Pete was heavy into concentration and needed no distraction. I turned to look back at Frank and give him the okay sign with my thumb and finger in a circle. He did not smile and kept following Pete's example, all the while coming closer to our boat. Trying to ride in our wake, he was only twelve feet behind us.

Climbing the waves one at a time, Pete skillfully worked our boat forward towards calmer seas. Finally I felt like we were going to make it. The rough waters lasted about twenty minutes, but it felt like a lifetime. The seas had wrapped mangled hands tightly around our boat and seemed reluctant to give us up. The last ugly wave tossed us up and into a quieter, safer wave and the calmer waters surrounded us. Frank was now able to control the distance behind us and slowed down to an acceptable pace. In his future stories he would often tell how lucky he had been to ride in our wake that day. I don't think he ever realized how close to crashing into us he had come.

One by one the other yachts limped into Bowan Island. Many of the skippers' wives were crying and I remember giving out many hugs as I tried to sooth raw nerves and relieved expressions. In the evening as we all sat around a cozy bon-fire as the stories of the day's crossing unfolded. The larger vessels, 40 to 45 feet had taken the worst wear as they were unable to crawl up and over each wave as the smaller vessels had. Our "Coralee" was 32 feet, Frank's boat was 28 feet, just the right size to fit into the saddle of the wave. Many skippers claimed this was the shortest but worse crossing they had ever done. The insides of these larger vessels looked like a "bull in a china closet" with contents of drawers and cupboards strewn across the galleys. One forty foot vessel had lost an engine and with wife at the helm had been lucky to make it. The port captain raised his glass to toast our adventure, "Here's to only fourteen miles!" No one raised a glass. No one smiled.

My Friend Nancy

My friend Nancy lived next door to me in Baudette, Minnesota. Baudette was a town famous for fishing, hunting and gossip. The most exciting thing to do was the movie on Saturday nights for 25 cents with free popcorn and the Moose Hall Dance on Friday nights that the whole town of 400 people was invited to attend, children and all. Because the climate in Baudette was so severely cold in the winters, next door neighbors made perfect playmates. Walking across town to a friend's house was an ordeal after dressing in three layers of clothes to brave 20 degree below zero weather and walk through snow drifts that varied from 3 to 5 feet tall. Having Nancy right next door was great.

Nancy and I walked to grade school each day in freezing weather with only our eyes peeking out of our face scarves. We wore double mittens with strings that ran through our jackets. Our insulated boots went to our knees. We loved to play outdoors even in the coldest of temperatures. We waited until our cheeks, nose and fingers were almost frozen before going inside. I remember standing in front of the wood stove so my body would thaw out. Our favorite activities were sledding, ice- skating, and making angels by lying on our backs and swishing our arms up and down to form angel wings. On the weekends the adults would build bon fires on the Rainy River, drive their cars out on the ice and roast hot dogs and marshmallows. Our house was on a hill overlooking Rainy River and all of us kids would pile on my toboggan on the front porch and ride down three hills that all went straight down to the river - the toboggan would drop and plop over each hill and then fly through the air at the bottom and across the river. We would all scream and hold on to each other and sometimes someone would get hurt if they didn't hold on tight enough and keep their fingers and toes above the snow and on the toboggan. What a thrill this was. Nancy and I had many a scream together.

Nancy was a quiet, shy person with an only brother. She loved hanging out with me because my house was full of noise from a family of eight. We were her second family and sometimes my mother would say our first family because she spent so much time at our house. Nancy had her own playhouse, built by her Dad, in her backyard. In the summer we would play "dress-ups" in her playhouse and walk to town in our outfits. In 1950 we knew all the adults in town were our friends and we would parade through town in our long gowns and hats and the local store owners would give us treats. Sometimes we dressed my three brothers, Mark, Les and Herm, in frilly dresses with lace, sat them in my red wagon and took them all downtown with us. Everyone is town knew us and would pretend we looked cute and indeed we thought we were gorgeous looking damsels.

Sometimes Nancy and I liked to get really dirty. On a hot summer day a favorite sport was jumping in the local cow pies outside of town in the pastures. We would look for the freshest pie, run and slide across it. Sometimes we fell and needless to say smelt pretty ripe by the time we returned home. One pasture had an ornery bull that we liked to tease; when the bull would run after us we would scramble up the fence as fast as we could go and laugh and laugh. I remember every inch of Baudette, Minnesota from the railroad tracks to the farm lands and cemetery. The whole town was our playfield and we had no fear for our safety in those days.

In 1998, my husband and I drove across Canada, through Winnipeg and into Baudette. I wished to show my husband the town I grew up in and indeed, I was able to walk to my old house from downtown the way I remembered. Nancy no longer lived next door. Her Dad had died, her Mom was in assisted living and her brother had his own auto repair shop. We stopped by to visit with Nancy's brother Donny and he said Nancy was married and living in Tucson, Arizona. What a surprise! We also lived in Tucson in the winters so I planned a lunch reunion with Nancy upon arriving in Tucson. The little girl play friend had changed a lot and so had I. We found we had little in common, our conversation was awkward and I haven't seen Nancy since.

My mother always said "Careful what you wish for." Sometimes childhood friendships are best left as memories.

Gabby

I had not planned to have a foreign exchange student living with our family in 1986. I already had two teenage daughters ages 16 and 17. Why would I want a third? And to top it off, Diana (that's me the parent) spent my day at the high school teaching English and Math to teenagers. I was already surrounded by hormonal madness and felt that I was teetering on the edge.

But things were about to change. Sharon, my youngest daughter, excelled in her Spanish class and had befriended Gabriella, a foreign exchange student from Tucaman, Argentina. Gabby, as we affectionately called her, bonded tightly with Sharon and became a daily visitor at our house. Soon, I received a call from Bob Branson, Gabby and Sharon's high school counselor. Bob and I were old friends and often helped each other solve teen-age problems, but little did I know that Gabby and Sharon were hatching a scheme that was about to happen. Bob explained to me that Gabby was in a sad position with her foster family who treated her as a baby sitter for their young children. Gabby said she was going back to Argentina or she would stay if she could move in with Sharon's family.

Aha! I should have seen this coming. So after the foreign exchange department screened our family and we signed as the legal guardians of Gabby, she quickly moved in with us.

Spanish became a second language for all of us and we all became language communication experts over night. Now, I must back up and explain the Argentine culture. Gabby grew up in an upper class neighborhood where the lower uneducated class was expected to serve the upper class, sort of an "upstairs-downstairs" life. Gabby's parents had a live in cook and house keeper. Thankfully Bob had explained this to me so I knew that expecting Gabby to do the daily chores was out of the question. Oh well, I couldn't get my own teenagers to do daily chores without a squabble or threat. My husband Peter came to the rescue. The poor man was now living with four women and had a different idea - hire a house keeper." So we did. She came once a week which helped us live in a somewhat cleaner environment, enabling us to spend more fun time with each other and less squabbling.

The Argentina visitor in 1986 became a change agent for our family in many ways. Gabby had been taught to say, "I have a problem" whenever she was confused or sad. So every day at least once and sometimes three times we heard "I have a problem." Life would stop when Gabby had a problem and we would we help her solve this problem, usually a language interpretation, but sometimes major that had to do with boys or school. We had taught our own children to take care of their own problems and needlessly our own daughters were self reliant but through the years had become more secretive and aloof. By helping Gabby solve her everyday problems we shared more of our own problems and became a closer family.

Gabby brought many gifts to our family that year. At bedtime she had been taught to always hug your Mom and Dad. Every night she would faithfully seek us out and give a hug of appreciation and love. This was an Argentina custom we adopted for our family. By accepting Gabby's differences we grew as people who like and appreciate differences in others. The following summer Gabby returned to her own family in Tucaman.

Over that same summer we received a call from the foreign exchange department at Hazen High School. Gabby's parents had called and wished to have Sharon stay with them for a year as a foreign exchange student. Again we got a call from Bob Branson, filled out all the paperwork, and Sharon spent her junior year at a high school in Tucaman, Argentina, living with her dear friend, Gabby. And, yes, there is another story about Sharon's visit to Argentina.

Grandfather

The gentle grey giant sat in his oversized, overstuffed grey leather chair pushing his pen across the margins of his papers. Beneath his feet the three year old granddaughter, snow blonde, puffy cheeks, and silver blue eyes, pretended to focus on her basket of home-made cotton dolls. The dolls were well-worn like her grandfather, missing a button eye, loose at a seam where the stuffing poked out, a bald spot of hair where a tuff of yarn used to be. She never really liked the dolls but dearly loved her grandfather whose presence was an honored privilege. She liked to stay put until his work was done.

Grandfather was still dressed in his formal teaching attire, grey suit with grey vest, white dress shirt with a button-up collar and cufflinks which read the initials of St. Cloud Teachers' College. John C. Cochrane, Lola's father, was the department head of all the history classes and had a reputation for great lecturing, keen memory, and fair grading practices. He enjoyed leisurely reading the essay papers required by his students. From seven to nine each evening was his quiet work time for reflection and writing. Having his loving granddaughter, his very first, living in his large Victorian house brought joy to his heart. Diana was the only child in the house, a precocious, curious child who constantly talked, asking hundreds of questions but not at this time - not in the evening during paper grading time. He took another purposeful puff from his pipe, paused -and then blew lazy circles in the air. Grandfather and granddaughter glanced upwards, watching the circles disintegrate into the larger hazy smoke layer above his head.

Diana glanced at her grandfather often as his pen seemed an animated object - moving swiftly in a curvaceous dance. Grandfather's mouth would frown sometimes and other times smile. He would talk to his granddaughter about his students' papers as though she was an adult who understood his language of a doctorate degree. And so, the love of a writing pen slipped inevitably through the Cochrane genes. At times, the grandfather gave an all-knowing smile as he instinctively knew she desperately wanted his pen and papers - and certainly not the dolls. He also knew she would have to wait until the magic began in first grade, when she received the large block lined penmanship paper and pencils.

The Afterthought: At age five my parents and I were living at grandfather's house in St. Cloud, Minnesota. We had occupied the servants quarters on the third floor with an upstairs-downstairs staircase winding centrally and secretly from the kitchen to the bedrooms. Grandfather's house was a magical place - parlor, pantry, cellar, attic, places to roam freely and play hide-and-seek with the cousins during the holidays. Lola, Diana's mother, was expecting her second baby. Les, Diana's father, was attending his final year at St. Cloud Teachers' College on the G.I. Bill. After WW II ended, money and jobs were scarce for the returning soldiers, so extended families shared their houses. This was a very busy time for my parents, who had little time for me, but my grandfather made time for me and often took me to college with him to walk the campus and visit with the professors and students. I was eager to go to school and my grandfather understood my needs. He talked to my parents about starting me in school a year early. My birthday fell on November 28th and the cutoff date was October first to enter first grade. He got his way which was my way and marched me off to first grade the first day of school. Of course, he knew all the teachers and he glowed with pride as he introduced me as his granddaughter.

As I reflect on this story, I realize that my grandfather shaped my values in education and literature. He was my beginning. He taught me to respect paper and pen and to foster my intelligence. The Cochrane genes are still flowing freely through my writings. The faint aroma of pipe tobacco still lingers in the air.

Grandparents To The Rescue

Seven o'clock AM the phone is ringing. "Mom, I'm sick, says a croaky, hoarse voice, "can you come a day early?" I do not function well without my first cup of coffee of the day, but I knew this must be a true emergency, so in my not awake voice I say, "of course. We'll be there as soon as we can." Wide awake now, I saunter down the hallway, feeling my way to the thermostat to push the heat lever up to 70. Feels like 35 in the house, so I climb under the heating blanket, snuggle butt to butt next to 6'2" of human warmth. Pete is also awake and anxious to pack the car and leave. Rolling over to catch more sleep is not going to be an option. I am having visions of daughter Susan trying to diaper and feed the babies, while feeling sick and probably coping with a sleep deprived night. Placing glasses on my nose, I head for the kitchen for the comfort of my coffee pot. Tuesday has become Susan's day instead of mine.

By nine AM, we are on the road. Grandparents to the rescue. Normally we spend Wed and Thurs with the grandchildren, babysitting while Johnny and Susan have a date night and catch up on their work errands. Both parents have full-time day jobs. Add two babies to their lives and you can get the picture. Although Susan manages her coffee business from home and has nanny help when needed, her A type personality keeps her on her feet even when sick. But let's face it, no one wants to care for a sick mother with two babies in diapers and bottles. Except the willing grandparents of course.

It takes one and a half hours to drive from LaConner to Fall City, stop at Susan's espresso stand for refreshments and unload the car. Sammy is at the door - "Nana. Papa," he yells and falls on the floor with his feet bending backwards like fresh-caught fish flopping about. Devon is scooting around the kitchen in her latest noisy toy on wheels. Devon is only six months but already a busy girl - rolling over, spitting, and cooing with loud, unlady like sounds. Sam is a little helper and helps unload our stuff to the guest room. He knows our routine and dearly loves the small cooler which he takes to the kitchen. Sam helps me unload our survival food - crackers, cheese, apples and bananas. At 22 months Sam is the constant Myna bird, aping every word we say. All day long I feel like I'm in an echo chamber. Must say I have certainly cleaned up my vocabulary!

Susan has made a doctor appointment and is out the door to the local medical clinic. She hopes for a miracle drug that will put her back on her feet in a hurry. Soon she is back home and her Dad, Pete is off to the drugstore to fill her prescription. Diana takes care of the two babies upstairs in the family room while exhausted Susan retreats to the safety of her own bed. Relief is on her tired, washed out face. Soon she is in a deep sleep.

At two a-clock PM, Sam and Devon both go down for afternoon naps. I check on the third baby in the house, my daughter Susan, who looks peacefully sound asleep - probably the drugs. Pete has heated hot water for two apple ciders and we sink into the soft brown well-worn couch for an afternoon of Lou Dobbs and Wolf Blitzer. Grandparents to the rescue brings contentment and feels like the right thing to do.

Hair-cuts

The Northwest Hair Academy in Mt. Vernon is a feast for my nose. The smells are a combination of a floral shop and a mortuary. As I approach the appointment desk, my nose tells me that tinting, perms, and shampooing are all underway. Today I am here for my monthly haircut. Laura looks up and says, "Do you have an appointment?" (Always a tedious question I am thinking - what else would I be here for, but I need to be cooperative as this is a school where students are being trained in reception skills.) "Yes, I have an appointment for 10:30 for a hair-cut." Laura replies, "Please have a seat and I will let the student know her client is here." She picks up the microphone and shouts, "Michelle, your client is here."

Sitting comfortably in the waiting room, I skim through the latest fashion magazines, looking at teen-age mod hairdos on thin heavily made-up faces. Feeling my age of 65, I am surrounded by mostly teen-agers from the local high school and the twenty-something young people from the Oak Harbor Air Base. I like being around these eager-beaver young learners. The mood is musical and up beat and the hair-dos are right out of "Hairspray", "Jesus Christ Superstar," and "The Hollywood Canteen." Colorful rainbows of hair capture my eyes and I am imagining what I would look like in purple or pink hair. Would be fun if I lived in California or Arizona, but in LaConner, conservative is the boring but accepted thing to do.

Across from me are shelves of Paul Mitchell products and I have purchased many of these to give me the young, clamorous look to no avail. Yet I love the scents -the coconut shampoo, the jasmine gel, and the pungent pure bleach-like smell of my latest new product called "Quick-Slip" which gives my hair its whipped-up messy look. A student walks over to the desk and asks, "Does

Michelle know her client is here." "Yes," says Laura but I know this is not a good sign; Michelle is probably out in the back alley having a cigarette, wolfing down a late breakfast, or taking too much time to set up her station. Oh, Oh, I am thinking. I have gotten "The Late Starter." Might as well relax, my twenty minute haircut has just turned into an hour.

The Northwest Hair Academy has three types of hair stylist, The Late Starter, The Piranha, and the Professional. The Piranha will devour your hair as fast as she talks. Snip. Snip. Lip. Lip. Whack. Whack. Chat. Chat. Making three trips around your hair, you will get three haircuts for the price of one. Sitting in stunned silence, you cannot stop the Piranha, for she is on a mission - a scissor happy hippy, crazy with the snipping. The Professional is my favorite for she cares about what the client wants and asks lots of questions, even holding up a lock of hair in her fingers to mark with her scissors what she believes to be exactly ¼ of an inch. "Is this how much you want cut off?" she asks. Oh how I love the Professional -so trustworthy and predictable. However, this is not my day to get The Professional. Michelle is standing over me with her purple hair, saying, "Are you Diana?" Faithfully, like a puppy, I follow her to her station to begin the slow process of getting my hair cut.

Her station is well organized with lots of extras. Three combs are lined up in a row. A spray bottle with warm water is close by. She excuses herself to go for a towel and black half circle cape for me. After draping me to protect my clothes, she wanders off to find her instructor who must approve the plan to cut my hair, which hopefully will be my plan also. I have said that I want a trim- only 1/4 inch off. Her hair has the mod cut of different lengths, some with purple blobs at the bottom clumps. Now the instructor is towering over me, asking Michelle to describe how she will cut my hair. "Just a trim," I remind them both. They exchange the glance that says I probably don't know what I want and continue lifting up patches of my hair to examine the texture as though they are experts pouring over a mysterious Petri dish. After their careful examination and conversation of haircutting, the instructor signs the student's form, allowing the student to begin my haircut. Michelle picks up comb number one and parts my hair into sections, neatly bunching each section up with clips, and reaches for the spray bottle. After loosening the section in the back, combing this gently into separated strands, she waters down the clump, and starts a careful snip, snip process that sounds like she knows what she is doing. I ask, "Are you close to graduating, Michelle?""Yes, only two months to go," she replies. Gradually I feel confident and safe to be Michelle's client. The comb drops to the floor and Michelle calmly reaches for the second comb. We both know the second comb will probably hit the floor also. Otherwise, why would there be a third comb? We continue with a polite see-saw conversation of small talk and eventually I am following her to the reception area to pay for my eight dollar cut. I give her a smile, a thank you and a three dollar tip. Tucking away her tip money into her black uniform, she heads for the back alley for another smoke.

The Heirloom

I was born in 1960 to a large cedar tree in the Olympic Forest. Not in the human sense of course as I was carved, polished and lacquered to a shiny cherry-wood finish. When my lid popped open a fresh heavy cedar odor filled up an entire room. I knew I was destined to a life of dreams and hopes. And here I am with another new owner who loves me like a brother. I am learning so many new things from Samuel and all his toys. I have a belly full of legos, trains, blocks and balls and here comes something new from the Christmas Day - a brand new Bob The Builder CD. Sam is only 20 months old and already he lifts up my lid and fills me up with the most amazing toys. Some days he decides to empty me out and start all over again. Everything is a game to Sam. I can't see him but I hear his giggles and talk all day long. This upstairs room where I live is filled with family sounds - I hear Susan puffing away on her exercise machine. Sam is learning new words so he shouts out every object he sees on television - fish, ball, water, etc. I do believe the large screen television set is a great teaching tool - especially the PBS SPROUT station. I reside in the family room with smells of popcorn and dirty diapers.

Baby sister, Devon, is only six months old and cannot lift my lid yet - she can't even crawl or walk so Sam will have me all to himself for a while longer. The day will come when Raggedy Ann will share a space with Bob the Builder. The feminine stuff will come flying in and I'll have to behave as an equal opportunity employer. I was originally owned by a girl so life goes full circle for me. Anyway I can't complain, I will outlive all my owners. This is the 3rd generation for me.

Okay! Okay! I started this story about my birth in 1960 and skipped right over to 2007. It's just that I'm having so much fun with the children and toys that it's hard to record my story but I know the future generations will want to know so I'll start at the beginning. In 1960 I was an engagement gift to Diana from Peter. Back then I was called a "Hope Chest" -not a toy box. I was brand new and filled with useful linens like sheets, towels, and special hand-embroidered pillow cases. As the years went by during Pete and Diana's marriage I rested peacefully at the bottom of their king-sized water bed in a suburb, Renton, Washington. No one ever took notice of me and I was only occasionally opened as more miscellaneous beddings were stuffed inside my chest. I was always full to the top and could hardly breathe. In 1985 Pete and Diana wished to buy a larger house with brand new :furniture - keeping up with the Jones I thought. Seems I didn't fit into their new decor so they sat me in the garage for further disposal to Goodwill. Goodwill for whom? I am thinking. The garage was dusty, dirty and crowded with junk. No one saw my tears.

But I was rescued by Daughter Susan who thought I was still beautiful and needed a chest for storage. Yes, from 1985 to 2001 I belonged to Susan and she treated me very well. I moved to Fall City, Washington and was placed at the end of her bed in the upstairs of a newly remodeled bedroom with all the extras, including a woodsy view. I blossomed into happiness. Her linens were more luxurious than her Mother's and I swelled with pride at all the colors and laces. So this is what upscale means, I am thinking. But in 2001 I had a very bad year. Susan got a divorce and put me into a public storage place. Locked me up in the dark and left me for weeks. Totally abandoned, I became depressed and again no one saw my tears! Little did I know the best was yet to come.

Susan remarried and moved into an even bigger house and found the perfect spot for me inside a soon-to-be children's room. Susan and I were pregnant and my happy hopeful chest was filling up with baby clothes. By now my cedar smell had faded and I became a handy box for the extra stuff like clothing, toys, and shoes. Susan just filled me up with whatever was her whim at the time. But after the babies were born, she decided I would be the upstairs toy chest. Soon I had competition in the house. The kitchen has a toy chest and the front room has a toy chest. But Sammy favors me over the others because I have Thomas the Train and Bob the Builder, his treasured toys. Sam and I are getting along quite well these days. He raises my lid gently and doesn't stuff me too full. The upstairs toy room has the new smell of a baby girl - feminine lotions and bubble spice. Devon will be my new owner someday and perhaps I will be at the foot of her bed as she fills me with her treasures. After all a "Hope Chest" must have HOPE.

P.S. - On the Internet a Lane Hope Chest is described as the most striking time capsule for preservation of your cherished memorabilia. I am still available in cherry wood. (41 x 15 x 20.5 for $349.00)

How to Fold a Sock

"Diana, what are you doing?" shouted my mother. The translation of this question was "I need your help, come quickly." And so I did, many times during the day. Lola was lucky to have a first-born child who loved to do household chores. In the 1940's I was a cleaning machine and had organization skills that far outweighed the other family members. I was not perfect of course. I hated kitchen cleanup which was a huge mess after eight people had finished eating and the cooks had slaved over their gourmet creations, which to me was a huge disorganized mess. "Diana, what are you doing," Lola's voice would shout after dinner.

My favorite chore was the laundry - sorting, hanging clothes on the lines to dry, folding, ironing, and stacking the neatly folded items in the dresser drawers. In the 1940's children were expected to pull their weight in a large family and I spent at least one hour a day after school doing laundry. Ironing was a favorite because I was paid a penny for each piece I ironed no matter how small or large the material was. Dad's handkerchiefs would create a quick stack of pennies, but a white sheet could take me 10 minutes so that was a slow penny. When I had accumulated 25 pennies, I had enough for the Saturday picture show.

My mother always had the latest washing machine from Sears Robuck but no dryer. In Northern Minnesota, we hung our laundry down in the basement on long out-stretched lines that crossed from one end to the other. Wooden clothes pins hung in a large bag on the line. The basement always had a damp, greasy smell like the inside of an auto repair garage. The clothes never smelled as good as the outdoor aroma of sunshine, bleach, and lilacs. When I hung the clothes on the lines outside in the summer, I would take my time. The new-born kittens would play at my feet and I would tease them with a long sock. Around and around they would prance, teeth fastened hard on the toe of the sock, determined to pull the sock away from me. When I let go, the kitten would tumble over and then run away with the sock.

In the 1950's we moved to a modern house with a laundry room. Lola had a newly purchased avocado Westinghouse washer and dryer. By now we were a family of eight and mother needed more than me to keep up with the laundry. The machines were not perfect. They came with a couple of thieves, who would often chew up a sock or two and then hide the sock where we never could find it ever again. We blamed this mischief on the sock mouse. But my mother was thrifty, and we didn't fold socks in those days we had baskets for our socks and often went to school with unmatched socks. Waste not want not was Lola's motto.

When I became a teen-ager I was glad to do my own laundry as I took pride in my daily dress. I certainly didn't want my white blouses, starched petty coats, and poodle skirts mixed among my three brothers dirty jeans and jackets. My sisters Pam and Flora were older now and could do the laundry chores so I mostly did the ironing which I was an expert at. I was now paid 25 cents an hour and soon became rich. "Why can't I do the ironing, sister

Pam would whine." "Because your older sister has more experience," replied Lola and the blush on my face would shine with pride.

By the time I left home in 1960, Pam and Flora had taken over the laundry chores. I had taught them my expertise of ironing. How to spray starch Dad's white shirt collars, how to rotate the white sheets under the too hot steaming iron, and how to fold the pleated skirts around the ironing board, using pins to keep the pleats in perfectly straight rows.

In 1963 I married Peter, so I had laundry for two. Many years passed by before Peter and I had our own washer and dryer so we used the local laundromat. We were both working so we did laundry on a Saturday or Sunday. We could put dimes in the machines and have all the laundry done in two hours while reading a novel or magazine. As we moved around in the 1960's we could always find a handy laundromat nearby. Peter had also done laundry as a child and was a willing helper.

When Pete spent four years in the Navy, he learned to fold his clothes a certain way - the Navy way. When he came home after his service years, he insisted we fold the corners of the sheets the Navy way which we now do to this day. One day when we were folding clothes together, Pete said, "Diana, I don't like the way you fold the socks." I gave him a brutal stare as I felt my face grow flush. A voice not quite my own came tumbling out of the hackles of my breath, a slow smirking raspy echo of words that said, "Well my dear, if you feel that way, I think you should fold your own damn socks from now on." Now Peter grew red in the face and said, "I would be happy to fold my own socks and I'll do yours also." The rest of the day went on with barely a word between us. We never folded socks together again. I always leave them in a pile and later he takes a meticulously amount of time to carefully match and roll each pair of socks.

In the 70's and 80's laundry machines came in all colors and could time your drying loads from 10 minutes to 70 minutes, creating a loud blast of noise like a tugboat whistle at the end. The evolution of folding socks or not-to-fold will continue. My grandchildren are learning to dress themselves at age four and five. At their house socks are thrown into baskets. Wearing unmatched socks is a common site. And no one even cares - not even Grandpa Pete who still does the Navy folds.

The Journey to Nowhere

Four police officers walked toward the crowd standing on the loading platform at the Mt. Vernon train station. The Amtrak train #510 was soon arriving to pick up passengers heading north. A stout large-boned officer said in an authoritarian voice. "People, we need you to go back inside the station." My friend Joann and I readily obeyed and stepped back inside the depot. We were hoping to watch this unexpected event but the train stopped well ahead of the loading platform as the officers walked south to board the train. We could only speculate. The security officer inside the depot explained that the officers were going to make an arrest on the train of "a person of interest."

This was our first day of travel on a three day excursion to Vancouver and Nanaimo, B.C. Not a great way to start the day, I'm thinking to myself. I had planned this trip and felt some responsibility for talking my friend Joann into accompanying me. I had traveled this trip many times by myself and the connections to train, bus, and ferry boat had always worked like clockwork. "A super easy trip" I had told Joann. "Just bring your passport and 100.00 Canadian cash and you will be all set." I had purchased the tickets a month early so we had qualified for the discounts. I pride myself on travel plans and had researched all the procedures in advance.Could this arrest of "a person of interest" be an omen of things to come?

The train was a half hour delayed out of Mt. Vernon. Riding the train is always delightful as we can walk around and buy snacks from the bistro. The landscape viewing out the window was not the best as it was a drizzly, foggy morning on July 26th 2011. The two and a half hour ride gave us plenty of time to catch up on our visiting. Our friendship has lasted thirty years so far and hiking together, traveling together, and meeting for lunches has kept our friendship growing. We keep tabs on each other and there is nothing we cannot share as we vent about our relatives, politics, and general state of world events. Joann is fun to travel with as she is flexible and takes things in stride. Little did we know how flexible we had to be on this trip.

I had planned a gourmet lunch at a French crepe restaurant in downtown Vancouver, B.C. during the two hour layover between train and bus. As the train pulled into "the cage" under the barb-wired fence the conductor gave instructions on the loudspeaker. "The Canadian Customs has new rules that we must follow so you cannot leave your train car until the car in front of you goes through customs first." This was the summer peak travel season, the train was completely full and we were sitting in the last car. Forty minutes later we were permitted to detrain and get in line for Customs. That left only 40 minutes until we needed to board the Greyhound which departed at 1:30 pm. Luckily the Main Street Station has a McDonalds so we headed for the unwanted fast food experience, ate quickly and got in line for the Greyhound. When I ride on a bus, I always ask for the seat up in front behind the driver, as I get car-sick. So we had the best seats for the scenic view. As I am telling Joann about the lovely ride through Stanley Park and across Liongates Bridge, the bus pulls out and goes the opposite direction that I remember. Now I'm worried we are on the wrong bus so I ask the driver. "No, Miss, you are on the right bus, we just go out to the freeway, during the summer, as that is the quickest route." I think my friend Joann is wondering whether this was a trip to take or not. I'm thinking that I am through with my travelogue. What could possibly happen next?

As we arrive at Horseshoe Bay to connect with our BC ferry to Nanaimo, the bus winds down the steep hill to a parking lot. "Okay, folks, everyone gets out here. Go inside the terminal and exchange your ferry ticket for a boarding pass. A Greyhound will pick you up on the other side and take you to the depot." I am completely confused at this point. The last time I took this trip the bus drove unto the ferryboat and off on the other side. Now I'm following the driver back to the bus, saying, "Why aren't we boarding the ferry on the bus?" "Because the Greyhound cannot afford the new ferry fees - we have to make money, not lose money." Joann and I take the long walk through the maze of switchbacks to the main terminal. The building was brand new, full of tourist shops and fast food restaurants. Next we get in line to trade our ticket for a boarding pass and walk directly onto the standing ferryboat. No waiting around here - I smile.

The huge three story ferryboat has many comforts and we travel for two hours across the Georgia Strait. The sun casts a shimmer of lazy ripples across the ocean and we are mesmerized by its spell. We find a window seat and look for seals, whales and other vessels. We both drift into afternoon naps, looking forward to the hotel room and a seafood dinner on the waterfront. We arrive in Nanaimo at four o'clock and walk outside to the bus parking spot. Other people that travelled with us are doing the same. After a 20 minute wait, I ask another traveler why the bus isn't here? She says because we showed up early and the bus won't be here until five a-clock. Seems we rode across on an earlier ferry that was running two hours late. If you ride ferries frequently, you will understand that sentence. Most ferries do not run off the clock, but depend on tides, currents, and people loading which are all unpredictable. Joann and I no longer care about time and schedules and head back to the ice cream shop for tasty chocolate cones. We find a bench in the sunshine, settle-in, and wait patiently for our bus. The bus is on time and takes us to the depot, which is the lower floor of the Howard Johnson hotel where we will stay for two nights. I tell Joann that I know the secret back entrance to the hotel. "Just follow me," I say. As I open the double doors into the hallway, we enter a tube of inky darkness. The doors slam behind us. Joann says, 'I can't see anything!" "Don't worry," I reply and grab her arm. "I know the way, just down the hall to the lobby." Further down the hallway we see a faint light in the distance. The chatter drifting towards us is talk about no electricity available due to the broken transformer which was hit by a car. Joann and I start to laugh, the hysterical silly laugh that says we can't take any more surprises. Ha! Ha! The hotel manager lets us check into our room, which is located close to the lobby. We have enough daylight in our room to do the essentials before heading outside to enjoy a walk to the waterfront just three blocks away. By now, we have both "really lost it" but are still looking forward to a leisurely seafood dinner. Approaching the Boathouse fine dining restaurant, we see only darkness and a note is posted on the front door. Now we are aware of how large this power outage really is. We look down the boardwalk and see no lights on any shops and hardly any people. We are hungry and determined to eat even if we have to beg something from one of the well lit up yachts on the docks. We keep walking south, past the closed shops. "What is that smell," Joann asks. "I think its fish and chips," I reply. Let's check it out." A small shack-like diner is floating on the water close to the docks. Year round xmas lights hang from the eaves - brightly lit in green, gold, and white. Then we hear the drone of a nearby generator. People are lined-up at the only food place available. A sign says "Best Fish and Chips on the waterfront." And so it was!!

Just a Loaf of Bread

Pete and I were on our way to a church seminar on a sunny Tuesday evening, seven O'clock. The topic was "The Changing Roles of Men and Women." We were both hoping this seminar would help save our marriage as we were floundering on the marital rocks of middle age and the sex role changes of the seventies. I wanted out of the kitchen and into a meaningful life that included a new career with brain challenges. Pete just wanted things to stay the same. He liked the role of chief breadwinner and living with the full-time home maker - that was me. My daily thinking had slid into home wrecker, not homemaker. So, here we were trying to learn something new from our minister, Rev. Heer, about survival in this new world, where men were becoming nurses and telephone operators, and women were becoming engineers and machinists.

On our drive to the church we would pass Albertsons, my neighborhood grocery store and I asked Pete to stop so I could run in for a loaf of bread. "Okay," he said, and parked our 1973 GMC truck right in front so I could make a quick dash in and out. Well, sad to say, nothing was quick about this stop.

After the automatic door slid back into place, my stiletto heels clicked noisily down the shiny tiled floor. "Oh! Oh!", my brain said to my slowing down robotic body. Something strange is happening here. Where are all the customers? Why is the store so quiet. My senses became acutely alert and I began to feel a drizzle of sweat down the middle of my back. I started to look around the store and as I looked up toward the front, I saw one lonely cashier filling a brown paper sack for a large man hovering over the cash register. "Oh, shit", my brain said to my slowing down robotic body. "This is not good." I began to feel alone and out of sync. My feet had landed on center stage, but the actors were mute - the play was on pause. I had entered the scene of a robbery in progress. I absolutely did not know what to do and I was afraid to move. Fear was taking over my thoughts, I noticed how afraid the cashier looked and decided my best move would be to walk cautiously towards the cashier so the robber could see me and not be surprised. Surprise scared me more than the sweat running down my back. "Excuse me, Mr. Psycho Bank Robber, but now that I have my loaf of bread, I will leave quietly out the front door or whatever you suggest. Ho! Ho!" Fear had gotten silly and why I felt like laughing at this point did not fit the picture. The cashier saw me coming down the aisle and with a wide-eyed look of fear, not just for my safety but for herself, pointed in my direction so the robber could plainly see that a reluctant shopper was on the loose. That would be me, with a loaf of bread dangling from my side.

At this point, I thought things were so awful, they couldn't get any worse. Wrong! While walking towards the cashier, I saw another man standing over the store manager who was kneeling in front of the store safe by the glass windows up in front. This man had a gun and looked like a no-nonsense, street wise druggie who probably was on the edge. I really didn't want to push either of these desperate robbers over the edge. Hey, they could have my damn loaf of bread. Not, funny, Diana, this is a serious matter here, not a time for smiling, joking, or laughing. Seemed like minutes before the robber told me what to do, in reality it was probably 30 seconds at the most. He said, "Go to the back of the store and lay down with the others. Stay on the floor for an hour and you will not be shot." My fear level dropped somewhat, because I had an assignment. My stiletto heels quickly moved towards the rear of the store, where a group of customers were lying face down side by side in front of the meat market. I quickly joined the bald-headed man on the end and no one said a word. I felt some comfort that I was now not alone and my fear could be cushioned somewhat into the cloud of fear hanging above the group. Certainly better to be here than be-bopping around the store. I laid the loaf of bread beside me.

Seconds turned into minutes and minutes turned into an hour. I heard police sirens and that was a good sign. I never heard a gun shot and that was a good sign. Patiently our group waited for the signal that it was safe to move. No one wanted to be the first to move. We stayed until a police officer came down the aisle and said, "Okay to get up. But stay put as we need to get statements from each one of you." "Stay put," I'm thinking to myself. Does he have any idea how badly I need a bathroom.

The air fills with conversations. Signs of relief and humor. (I do believe humor follows fear!) I would like to hug someone at this point, anyone would do. The bald-headed man looks like he could use a hug so I give him one, whether he wants one or not. "Feels good to alive, doesn't it", he says. "Yes it does," I reply, "And to hell with this damn loaf of bread!" as I throw it into the meats - between hamburger and pot roasts. Throwing things always made me feel better.

Not once during this dangerous situation did I think of my spouse who after dropping me off, had been witness to the robbery from outside the glass windows. But here he comes, the real person, Pete, and he grabs me in his arms and says, "Are you alright?" "I think so," I replied but notice that my hands are shaking and my legs so weak that I am lowering myself to the floor. We both sit on the floor and talk and talk about the last hour of events, the verbal lava flowing quickly from the mountain of relief and mixed emotion. Who cares about the changing roles of men and women, I'm thinking, feels good just to be alive!

LaConner Town Government 1933-1943[1]
Milo Moore Mayor

In 1933 a special town caucus was held sponsored largely by volunteer firemen to nominate a fireman to run for Mayor and to enter the names of two firemen to run for the town council. The election stirred up the entire town's people, with a group of firemen attempting to unseat the older dominate citizens of the town. They did it, with Mayor Milo Moore wining by seven votes and the other firemen with about the same margin.

1 Copied from the Puget Sound Mail, 1943

In 1933, we were in the midst of a Depression. There were few jobs, the town business was not thriving with two fish canneries, with the price of salmon (Pink at 5 cents each, Chum sold to buyers at 10 cents each, and King about 5 cents per pound.) About all the young folks had was plenty of salmon to eat, home brew, and local fruit and vegetables. Farm workers were paid $30.00 per month room and board.

The town funds were very low. As Mayor I appointed Milo Caple, the one and only policeman at about $70.00 per month. The major and firemen helped him out when he needed help. Also, Matt Jarbo, a retired Army officer served as town marshal with his pay being less than $100.00 per month. We had plenty of action with fights and drunks. Yet, most town problems were manageable, with the help of the County Sheriff and with the aid of our County Commissioners guarding our streets.

Early in my assignment as Mayor, working in the County Treasurers office with Treasurer George Dunlap, the town of LaConner managed to purchase a small building that went for taxes next to the LaConner Co. Maple Dance Hall. It was on this lot the town built a Fire Hall and city council meeting location. The town borrowed $3,700.00 from G.O. Moen, Skagit Investment Co. on promissory notes payable in three years. This fund paid for lumber and items, not donated, and the firemen built the Fire Hall with donated labor. The firemen also gave clam chowder feeds to the public to raise money to build fire equipment. Alfred Nelson and Albert O. Nelson both at times were firemen and councilmen. They designed and built the Fire Hall, with the help of many volunteers. The town banker was so upset over the firemen being involved in town affairs, he would not loan the funds mentioned to purchase lumber, etc., but when the time came to insure the building he wanted the insurance account. Mayor Milo Moore said no to the council and would not sign the claim voucher. We gave the insurance to G.O. Moen who loaned us the money to complete the building.

A year or two after building the new Fire Hall, I and Bill Savage went to Seattle, called on Bill Conner to ask him if the Conner Estate would sell the Maple Hall (brick building) to the firemen. We told him we did not have much money and wanted to fix the building up for dances and install a bowling alley. Bill

Conner sold the building to the LaConner Volunteer Firemen for less than $500.00. We then had the Conner Estate deed the building over to the town of LaConner so we would not have to pay taxes. The firemen were not organized to do business owning real property. These two buildings were the town headquarters for many years. We kept the old City Hall for the Town Clerk, Water Department and jail.

Now getting back to some recent arguments on who owns the old fire hall in LaConner. There is no doubt that the building belongs to the town of LaConner. The Maple Hall by the town of LaConner title should recognize the firemen paid for the building, and for all I know have been in charge of this building all the years since its purchase. It has however been a useful part of the town enterprise. I believe the town is responsible for the upkeep and management of the same to some extent. There is a need to continue the good relationship with the LaConner Volunteer Firemen. If for some reason there is again a conflict between the town government and the firemen, they might again run their men for elected offices and once again assume control of the town operation.

About 1936-37 the U.S. Army Corps of Engineers began dredging the Swinomish Channel. They brought in the old steam dredge Missouri. They were pumping sand from the channel all along the channel shore. I talked matters over with Gene Dunlap and Jim Hulbert about filling sand around the park hill. I decided to go to Seattle again and talk to Bill Conner and family about getting title to the tide lands in front of the park which had been previously given to the town by the Conner Family. Bill said, "If it is alright with the rest of the family they would give the tide lands to the town of LaConner." They did, and working with the County Treasurers Office I discovered there was a special harbor improvement fund with several thousand dollars in it. This money was paid to the state by LaConner waterfront property leased in the harbor area. I contacted Representative Pat Hurley and Fred Martin, members of the Legislature, and they passed a bill allocating such funds as paid into the state for harbor leases from new towns of fourth class not already entered into a port district could now be paid to the town governments. This included LaConner, Coupville and Snohomish. By this act, LaConner got over $5000.00.

Gene Dunlap, Jim Hulbert and I talked with Ed O'Leary, District Surveyor for the U.S. Corps of Engineers, about getting the General Construction Dredging Co. to fill the old mill site and park area with sand. They contacted Colonel Frank Greeley, Head of General Construction, about this. I told him we did not have much money. He said he would do the job for whatever the town could pay. Jim Hulbert and Gene Dunlap had a drag line dredge and they built a dike around the tide lands for free. The tidal basin ran from the pea cannery south around the park to the area now under lease by New England Fish Company.

In all this operation Ed O'Leary gave his help to the town of LaConner without charge. He has served for some 40 years to aid in the development of LaConner waterfront without compensation, in so far as the work involved the town of LaConner.

After filling the tidal area in front of the park, we began to build a road around the area. I had a friend at Marblemount who was in the stone business. He gave me a large slab of granite which I hauled to Fretz Monument Co. in Mt. Vernon. Mr. Elsworth Fretz surfaced the granite slab and inserted the words, In Memory of Louisa A. Conner for whom this town was named and through who's generosity this park is yours to enjoy. Or words to this effect. We placed this monument at the base of the park area. Fretz Monument Co. did not charge for the work.

Some time later a Fish Cannery Co-op was formed and local people joined in the building of a fish cannery on land in front of the park under lease from the town of LaConner. Eventually the Fish Cannery Co-op went broke. I and my brother Vernon called upon Sam Alheddaf, Whiz Fish Co. in Seattle to buy the building and equipment from the creditors. They finally did for $9000.00 and set up a modern fish processing plant. It was paid for in the first two years of operation. As Mayor and one who signed the original lease, and the reassignment of the cannery lease to Whiz Fish Co., I stipulated that the buildings must be painted white and kept up in good order.

At this point I should mention I appointed Jim Hammack of Mt. Vernon our town attorney. He served well and had a strong interest in boating along our waterfront. He was paid $15.00 per month for his services. This helped his secretary with paper work on the town's behalf.

Just before the war broke out with Japan, the town made a lease for part of the town's tide lands just south of the New England Fish Cannery with C.O. Davis, where he built a shipyard and boat repair, marine ways operation. The town had previously built a marine railway with steel beams, etc. that came from the old bridge material obtained from Skagit County. I worked with the Davis Shipyard and finally took charge of this operation in 1944. I was doing quite well when in 1945 Governor Mon Walgran asked me to be Director of Fisheries.

In setting forth the filling of sand in the diked area in front of the park, we did this without making surveys. We followed the hill and dike to a southerly point which we were informed was the south end of the LaConner Co. tide lands. At the time we did hear of some mix-up in just where the Conner deed to the town was involved. The Conners had promised Axel Jensen some part that he had deeded to the town, but we never followed up on making a survey of the description of the deed involved.

I recall very plainly during my ten years as Mayor of LaConner that we did not have much revenue from taxes. We built roads, graveled roads, helped the Town Marshall and carried out many other programs without the use of public funds. Not once during ten years did I have opposition from the Town Council. We also had cooperation from the Mt. Vernon Fire Department when Chief Joe Slauncher gave us a fire hose to help with our fire department when we purchased a new truck. Not once did we over spend the town budget or have a special election to raise money for a public enterprise. The Town Marshal, Mayor, Water Superintendent, Councilmen and others gave their time to help the public without charge.

The Last Round-up

The tired old selfish man slumps in a corner in the dark dining room, hiding from sunshine and relatives. He wears a large floppy white cotton sunhat that covers his neck and ears. Gray white scraggly hair hangs unkempt over his ears, he thinks of his brother Leo who died from melanoma and blames the sunshine and too many cigarettes they smoked together as boys. Les is 84 years old, his body no longer works, his heart is failing and death is just around the corner. His thoughts are not healthy. He knows he is the next in the family to die and is afraid. He has much to atone for but he does not know how to ask for forgiveness. He has lived a whole lifetime and alienated all his children and grandchildren from him. His sick brain works on his depression and he thinks that only his black labs, well-trained to obey his commands, understand him. Dogs are so easier than people. I tried to control my children and my wife Lola, but they went their separate ways. I do not know how to hug a child or tell her that I Love her. Instead, I say hurtful things to get their attention. I point out their flaws. Fat, ugly, and stupid are my favorite words. But today I must behave myself as this is my last family reunion. Death is sniffing at my heels and I have nowhere to hide.

My son Herman has rented an old family cottage by Flathead Lake, Montana, July 4th weekend, 2005. I can tell that a happy family lived here by the cheerful pictures on the walls and educational magazines, books and puzzles scattered around the living area. The wood walls smell of warmth and love. The women gather in the kitchen preparing food. They laugh, hug, and tell family stories. I feel sad that I do not feel more love and warmth from my family. As I hear this noise, I sit quietly by myself in my self-made darkness. Even my second wife Eileen avoids me. She had kissed and played with Susan's new four-month old baby, Sam Walker. I could only watch from afar and tell Diana, the new grandmother and my oldest daughter that I don't like babies.

I told Susan that she was fat and she looked hurt and said, "I just had a baby, grandpa." I am even afraid of a baby. A new life begins as mine is coming to a close. I am angry about that.

Dallas, another old man in his eighties, my children's step father, sits at the picnic table on the deck and deals the cards. He teaches the new young children in the group how to play cribbage. He smiles and they smile and their laughter floats in the air. Real communication takes place and I am jealous. At another table sits a group playing Mexican Dominos. Pete and Sharon are teaching Les, Kim, Jeff, and Victoria how to play. Kim and Les smoke and drink too much. My son Les is in the late stage of alcoholism and I feel angry that I was unable to fix his problem. Lola divorced me when he was a teenager so my family of victims moved away from me.

Herman is taking people for sailboat rides but I am afraid to go. My legs are crippled and I can barely walk. I can not save myself if I fall in the water. Lots of activities are happening on the Flathead Lake - Lyam and Jesse are sail boarding, Sharon and Susan are out on the jet ski, Johnny is trying out a new kite that will take him 30 feet into the air so he can do somersaults and fancy turns. They are all so young and full of energy. Everyone is having a good time and feeling family-close but me. I would like to leave and go back to my house to sit with my Black Labs, the only animals that understand and love me.

My loneliness and stress is feeding my emotions. Suddenly, I know the answer to my dilemma; I will throw a fit, a rage of sorts to get everyone to focus on me. And this will be a release from all this volcanic lava flowing through my body. It is so unfair to be the only unhappy person at the family reunion. I will wait for dinnertime when we are all gathered on the deck and then I will seek revenge on the ones I love. How dare they all have all this fun without me!

But first I will eat the delicious dinner - steaks, baked potatoes, fresh string-beans from the garden, and ice cream for dessert. But chewing my food is so hard for me. Everything takes too long as I slice my meat into tiny pieces and wash my food down with the only half-glass of wine my doctor allows. People sitting close to me are quick to eat and move to another spot. Too much smoking and drinking so I am glad to see them leave. After dinner, I look for a smoker and Sharon comes into view. She leans on the railing with a fresh-lit cigarette held high in the air. How stupid she looks I think to myself, smoking in this high fire danger area. I will tell the others how stupid she looks. So I start my raging and it takes me over and makes me feel important. The group is looking at me now and I have a captive audience. I say I don't want to be here among all these stupid people and I am leaving. No one stops me from leaving. Herman, my youngest son, walks me to my car. He is concerned for my soul and talks to me about God and forgiveness. My wife Eileen is in tears and apologizes to everyone as we leave. My daughter Flora says good riddance. Once again I have upset the group. My goal has been reached. Everyone frowns and looks unhappy. I have made them pay for leaving me alone and having fun without me. I will go home to my dogs.

Aftermath

The next day on July 30th 2005, Saturday, the family tried to debrief from Grandpa's angry rage. Each son and daughter had suffered his abuse from time to time during their upbringing as children and later as responsible adults. Because they had experienced similar hurt in their lives, they were most sympathetic to Sharon, Susan and Diana and made sure to seek out each victim for a quiet discussion of what had happened to them in their lives from their father or grandfather's wrath. The stories ranged from true to humorous. Someone suggested we send him a carton of cigarettes for his birthday, which happens to be October 31st, Halloween, when most monsters are born.

Lots of excuses were made for his behavior. Flora said he was still recovering from his grief over his Brother Leo's death and didn't know what he was saying. Pam was so pissed she said, "I've had it with him. He'll have to do some apologizing before I let him back in my good graces." Herman felt bad that the outburst happened at his Family Reunion, being the gracious host that he was. Margaret said he needed his medication checked and maybe a blood test for Alzheimer's. Mark said he wasn't there and didn't hear anything. Kim said she was sad her kids had been exposed to such awful behavior and put-down language. Susan said she never had a relationship with the man so ignored his rude statements.

Dallas explained that he had been working up to a rage all week and was looking for an excuse to blow and maybe the boat dock fire in the neighborhood had pushed him over the edge. Lester was still recovering from his usual morning hang-over and fogginess so avoided talking to anyone. Herman and Diana said they didn't understand his behavior and admitted it was totally unacceptable.

Sharon was still hurt as she had tried to apologize for her smoking but her grandfather had turned his back on her on his way to his car. She felt it was her fault that he left. Sharon had been victimized the worst, but said she still loved him and forgave him.

The oldest daughter, Diana, was still upset upon returning home. Les, Senior, had been a terrible father, a worse grandfather and probably now an evil great grandfather. She was determined to protect her family in the future from his outbursts. Eileen, his wife, was still a precious dear woman and she would never cut her out of the family, but she wanted her Dad to know about the hurt he had caused and how she truly felt about his unacceptable rage which had been directed first to Sharon, then to Susan, and then to the group.

On August 2nd Diana had written two stories about her Dad's behavior at the Family Reunion, but still felt she needed to contact her Dad directly to give him an ultimatum. So she wrote her feelings on a post card, addressed to him only, to explain how hurtful his behavior had been to the family and that she and her daughters would have no further contact with him until he apologized. She meant every word and it felt good to take some action. She would wait and see if the mean old scrooge had the courage to contact her. But she was a survivor and didn't care if he called or not.

A Lifetime Friend

I would have never expected to develop a friendship with Joann Howe. It is strange how we make new acquaintances knowing a new friendship is just a passing moment. That's the way Joann and I felt about one another - just a passing moment in time. We had met on a hike on Tiger Mountain on an adventure with the Issaquah Hiking Club. She, of course, was the hike leader, trim and fit like a man just out of the weight room and I, not so fit and trim, trailed the group at the end. I was use to being the last person on the hike, short legs and thirty pounds overweight gave me an excuse.

I was feeling a little annoyed at the leader, Joann - making a mental note not to go on one of her hikes again. Sweating profusely I was struggling with the pace. When we reached the summit, we sat in a circle, sharing our lunch treats and discussing trivial events of life. Joann was a generous, caring sort of woman; she held the respect of all in the group. She was a Mountaineer and had hiked to the top of every mountain in the state of Washington, even Mount Rainier. I was never attracted to the rugged, outdoor types who made me well-aware of my unhealthy body. I joined the hiking club, because I knew I needed to get away from my desk, exercise, and lose the weight my doctor said I needed to lose. Also, I was fighting a high cholesterol level and was on a new medicine, Zocor. But my doctor had told me to drop the pounds and change my diet. Most of my hobbies had been sitting hobbies, like crossword puzzles, reading, writing and watching old movies from the forties. But, here I was, on top of a mountain exchanging small talk with a bunch of healthy looking people. Doesn't mean I have to enjoy this, I'm thinking to myself, as I pull out another bag of potato chips.

On the way down Tiger Mountain, Joann took the last place in line. To my surprise, this was the tradition of the hiking group. The leader would lead up the mountain and then follow last on the way down, making sure everyone was still with the group. So Joann stuck with me, taking her time on the trail, examining the sights and sounds of nature. She was an avid photographer and stopped to take pictures of the wildflowers and the fir trees with mossy hammocks draped in their branches. She was a woman in love with nature. I had never really met a woman of this sort and I became fascinated with her knowledge of flora and fauna. All the wildflowers had names and I realized I had much to learn about the outdoors.

As we talked the casual talk of strangers, we started to realize we did indeed have things in common. She had two daughters about the ages of my two daughters. She was struggling to save her marriage - me too. She and her husband, Bob, were visiting a marriage counselor; Pete and I were at the reluctant stage in our marriage - trying to decide to stay together or not. Joann had a full-time job as a manager at Fred Myers Dept. Store in downtown Renton. I was a high school principal at the Saratori School in downtown Renton, just one mile from where she worked. We were both balancing full time jobs, travel, and the difficult task of understanding our teenage daughters. By the time we finished the last four miles of our hike, we had learned a lot about each other. I knew then that I would do more hiking with Joann and that a healthy looking trim and fit friend was maybe what I needed at this time of my life.

Indeed, the more we hiked together, the more our friendship grew. I have learned a lot about nature trails from Joann and how healthy the outdoor life can be. There was literally nothing that Joann and I could not talk about and our ease with each other grew and grew. When Peter and I retired and moved to Arizona for the winters, Joann planned Arizona vacations with us and hiked all the mountain ranges around Tucson. Peter became Joann's friend also and we were a hearty threesome on the rocky, cactus, mountain trails. Joann's marriage did not survive like mine did but our friendship is as strong today as it was in 1980.

How does one keep a friendship going? We talked about this at one time and knew our friendship meant so much that we would make a commitment to each other and so we did. We never let a month go by without a get-together or phone call. This has worked to keep our friendship alive, even through the busiest months. Next Wednesday is Joann's 60th birthday and we will meet for lunch at Coho's in downtown Issaquah to reminisce about old times. Next April we have planned an exploratory trip to Salt Spring Island in Canada. I love to travel with Joann. We pack our hiking boots, outdoor clothes, and off we go - she likes spontaneous travel as I do and we delight in exploring a new town, island, or nature trail. This is a friendship that will never die.

Lester Franklin Blume (1924 - 2011)

Lester Blume was the father of Diana, Pam, Flora, Mark, Les, Jr. and Herman. Lola, his first wife was the mother of all the children. Les's second wife, Eileen, had no children but loved Les dearly and cared for him until his death in 2011 . As a father, he had been called many names by his children, including "the mystery man," the rude German, the man with a wall around him. Needless to say, his children had a hard time getting close to him. Les loved his children but had a sarcastic manner that kept his children from getting too close. I am Diana, the oldest, and I can honestly say that I know less about my father than I wish I did, but have never been able to ask the questions of him I would have liked to because he was always evasive to my curiosity. Sometimes he would say rude things just to build a wall between us or to "put me in my place." I always loved my Dad even though I did not understand him very well. And, I knew he loved me.

Les was born in Osakis, Minnesota to Edna and Herman Blume. He was the middle child, Leo was the oldest, and Wayne was the youngest. His father, Herman Blume, was a successful farmer who later became a salesman for John Deer tractors. Edna was a strong German lady who kept an immaculately clean house and knew how to stretch a dollar. Les had a strick upbringing, typical of a German household in the 1920's and 30's. After high school he joined the Army to serve in World War II During this time he met Lola, married her and started baby number one, that's me. After the war, Les used the GI Bill to attend St. Cloud Teacher's College and completed a Master's Degree in Math. Later Lola and Les moved to Baudette, Minnesota where Les had his first and only teaching job at Baudette High School.

As a small child growing up in Baudette, I remember my father mostly being absent from the family. To keep a large family in money, my Dad had to do many jobs. In Baudette, he was a math teacher, a football coach, ran the movie projector at the local theatre, and was cook and pilot on Rowell's yacht. When he was home, it seemed to have a negative effect on the flow of the household. Lola was always happy living in a cluttered environment with lots of children and animals running throughout the house. My Dad wanted a quiet , neatly organized house - everything in a proper place. Lola and Les definitely saw things differently from early on. As a small child growing up in a family of eight, I was expected to carry my load and help with the family chores. My father pointed out to me many times that I was the role model for my brothers and sisters, and needed to excel. I bought this mandate and worked hard to be the best at everything I did. When I failed, my Dad would let me know. He refused to sign my report cards unless I had all A's. He was proud of me when

I was successful but still a sharp voiced critic. I remember when I had achieved my high school principal promotion and my Dad said he was worried that I had such a large budget to account for and that I might not be able to handle this. His lack of confidence hurt my feelings, so I shot back, "I know what I'm doing, Dad, so give me a pat on the back instead of a kick on the but!" He would smile when I put him in "his place" and seemed to like me as an antagonist. We got along better when we were disagreeing than when in agreement. He once told me I was a challenging child and it annoyed him that I was so smart.

Lester's favorite lifetime hobby was raising, breeding, and showing Black Labs. He was well know as a judge at the dog trials. After his divorce in 1965, these black labs became his family. My mother, Lola, had taken the five remaining children with her to live in the city of Seattle. My Dad remained in Edmonds in a beautiful old historical house with a view of Puget Sound. The divorce between Lola and Les was full of bitterness and lies with never any reconciliation. All children were caught in the middle with negative comments coming from both sides. This was a most unhappy time for all of Dad's children. Les retreated from his children into a life of caring for his three dogs and traveling more often to pharmacies all over the Northwest. Les had given up a teaching position back in the 1950's to become a salesman for Rowell Laboratories. Of course he became the top salesman for Rowell and won many awards.

Les was not a very good father but he did love his children. I can only remember one time that my father invited me on a trip with him to Victoria and it was to a dog trial. My father would never call me up to say, "How are you?" and he seldom said "I love you" but I knew he did from an occasional hug or pat on the back. If I wanted contact with Les, I had to be the initiator. But I was very good at taking care of my own needs so I would call and stop by like a faithful daughter does. I was lucky to have other strong male mentors in my life like my Grandfather John Cochrane and my high school Young Life leader, Hal Thwing. These men showed me the sensitive, gentle side of maleness. Although my father was not the major role model for me, he instilled in me a strong drive for independence and the ability to be self-sufficient.

Lola Francis Cochrane - Blume (1921 - 1993)

Lola was a beautiful baby born to John and Francis Cochrane in St. Cloud, Minnesota. Lola's father, John Carl Cochrane had a Doctorate in History and taught history classes at St. Cloud Teachers College. Lola's mother, Francis Lola, was a homemaker and mother of five children; John, Junior, was the oldest, Bill, Flora, Lola, and Carl, the youngest. Francis Lola, Lola's mother, had also received a college education and had a Master's in Latin and Genealogy. Lola grew up two blocks from the college and in a household that fostered academic achievements. My mother always labeled herself the "black sheep" of her family because she was not interested in academic achievements and saw no need to further her education after high school. She reluctantly attended the local college for two quarters but dropped out in 1941 to marry my father Lester Franklin Blume and soon afterward Diana Lola, that's me, was born November 28, 1942.

Lola loved being at home, doing housework, baking cookies and homemade breads. I remember the house full of home baked smells, especially the cinnamon rolls right from the oven. Lola was a wonderful cook. My Dad was still in the Army in World War II when I was born, but after the war ended, Lola and Les and baby Diana lived with Lola's parents in St. Cloud, Minnesota. I remember how my grandfather, John, adored his first grand-daughter and would read me stories from his book collection. He took me on long walks around the college campus and introduced me to all the other professors. The college had underground tunnels from building to building and that was so fun to walk through. I remember the brown stucco house of my grandparents which was large with two bathrooms and five bedrooms, a front parlor, a pantry, basement, a dining room that would sit 25 people comfortably around a large oak table, and an attic so big you could walk around in it and play the old Victor records on the old Victrola record player with a wind up crank-handle. My favorite song was "I Have No Bananas." During this time, 1942-44, my father, Les, attended the local college and obtained a teaching degree in high school math.

My father's first teaching assignment was in Baudette, Minnesota, and this was the place my folks had their first house, all to their very own. I remember missing my grandfather after we moved but he wrote me letters and that helped. My mother loved her neighborhood in Baudette and often had the neighbor women in her kitchen for coffee and cigarettes. She had a washing machine in the basement, hung the clothes in the backyard (even in 20 degree below weather), and loved to sew and iron. Soon I had a baby sister, Pam, to play with and two years later another sister, Flora. Mother had her hands full with her three daughters, but she also wanted sons. Lola loved having babies and each baby became another play friend for me. Eventually I had 2 sisters and 3 brothers who all took the place of my dolls as I dressed them and cared for them like the older child often does. Indeed, my mother depended on me to be the second mother of the family and I felt much responsibility from an early age. My sister Pam was a big helper too. Pam liked to cook and I liked to do house chores so we helped Lola a lot. My Mom used to pay me one penny for each piece of clothing I would iron and when I had twenty-five cents saved I could see the Saturday night movie in town which was usually Roy Rogers or The Lone Ranger.

Lola's favorite sayings: "Remember I love you always, no matter what." "I hope you have a child just like you and then you will know what I have to put up with." "Does anyone know where Mark is?" (Mark was born hyperactive and no-one could keep up with him.) "Don't fall into a snow drift." "If you get bitten by a snake it won't be the snake's fault." "Be home before dark." My mother had a way of making her kids self-reliant at an early age. Lola taught us how to stretch a dollar by shopping for the best buys and making our own clothes out of hand-me-downs. I could take apart one of my Dad's wool suits and make a skirt and vest out of it. My mother's favorite vacation was a trip to the local state park where she set up a large tent and turned us six kids loose. We spent many summers at state parks with lakes. Lola said it was the best way to have fun with all of us. We could get dirty and then play in the water and eat hot dogs by the fire. Lola loved the outdoors in the summers and loved her kitchen full of friends and neighbors in the winters. She was happiest with a house full of people and lots of noise. Lola taught me how to make my own entertainment. I cut my own paper dolls from the Sears catalogue. I made doll houses out of cardboard boxes. Life in the 1940's was full of simplicity and laughter and Lola seemed like a child herself with a house full of babies.

For The Love of Books

My living room and dining room are filled with boxes of books. Such an unusual event is taking place. My daughter Sharon has two computers set up on the table; she is on a loving mission of researching old books - looking for the current price on E-bay and bookstore web sites. She bends over each book as though a golden treasure is in her hand and her search is a trip through Never Never Land. Some books are rare, others are classics, and some are precious coffee table books from family and friends. Sharon was a close friend of my neighbor, Jay Campbell, who loved Sharon from birth to her present age of 38 as though her own granddaughter. Jay passed away on January 10th 2008, one week before her 92nd birthday. Jay's family, two sons and one daughter, have been cleaning out the house, located across the street from us. It is now March and Jay's family is anxious to place the house on the real estate market.

Jay Campbell's most important hobby was her book collection. She had bookcases filled in every room and often listened to her favorite opera while reading an old classic. Sharon excelled in English Literature in high school and college and currently has a used bookstore inside Pioneer Coffee House in Cle Elem, Washington. Sharon's life is devoted to the love of books, as was Jay's. So here we are with all Jay's books inside our house with a great task ahead for Sharon. This is not a new experience for Sharon; other people have asked her to appraise their book collections and her amazing memory keeps the details of each book she has studied.

Her discovery has netted some amazing results. A Dickens Biography, 1949, will sell for $120.00. Books range in value from $5.00 to $30.00, from $125.00 to $450.00. A 1902 book, Breaking Into Society, by George Ade would sell for $30.00. A 1904 book, Sequil, by Henry Shute would sell for $25.00. Many of the coffee table books were about Northwest photography and international oil paintings and watercolors, all illustrated with high quality prints. Jay's family, including many cousins, arrived on March 15th and 16th to the final clean out of Jay's house. After sorting through the boxes Sharon had carefully marked, they took what they wanted and brought the remaining boxes of books back to our house to give to Sharon. Many of these remaining books will be donated to the LaConner Library, where they will sell for one dollar each in the Book Nook. Jay Campbell was a member of Friends of the Library all her life and had recycled many of her books through the years.

Ah! For the Love of-Books! Used books are like weathered old-growth oak trees that will live forever.

(P.S. Jay Campbell's ashes were scattered at Martha's Beach on March 16th, 2008 by her loving family, Gretchen, Ty, and Doug.)

The Neighborhood – 2012

The truth and nothing but the truth about my neighborhood is so much better than fiction. However, I will not use real names to protect the innocent or the not so innocent. The houses will be referred to as boxes and letters used instead of names. I shall begin with Mr. and Mrs. B who live in Box One. This couple uses their house as a cottage get-away on the occasional week-end. He collects classic cars, likes to make lots of noise with his hot engines, loud leaf blower, and lawn mower. No napping for us when Mr. B is at home. When visiting with him, he seems not to know when to stop talking, so one must find an excuse to walk away. Mrs. B likes to talk about her vacations to Europe and Hawaii. Her makeup and hair is always professionally done and she loves her little dogs which will be in your face when you visit with her. Their main house is in Bellevue in a new development two houses from where their oldest boy lives and their grandchildren. They once owned a successful heating and air-conditioning business but now are retired. We thought we would see more of them when they retired but not the case. Mrs. B once told me she could never live without her remodeled modern kitchen in Bellevue.

In Box Two live a family of seven people. The wife and husband are in their 40's but are living separate lives at this time. Mr. C is an engineer working in Afghanistan to help develop new infrastructure. When they all first moved in we had quite an adjustment to make. Mrs. C was pregnant with child five, the other smaller pre-school children ran the neighborhood with their two dogs, one older three legged dog and one obnoxious puppy who dug holes in my landscaped yard. The children loved to play in our ditches and still to this day arrange the rock piles which creates work for us. However, the two older boys are now teenagers, driving, and acting like the fathers of the family. They are the friendly sort and wave to us and bring us cookies during the holidays.

In Box Three live a very elderly couple, Mr. and Mrs. D. Both are retired writers who still publish their novels and poems. She is losing her eyesight and he has lost his hearing but they still do daily walks with their canes. Such a loving sight to see as they cuddle together to hold each other up on the way to the mailbox each day. Their house is for sale but in today's economy no one has looked at the place. They wish to move to the LaConner Retirement Inn but can't do so until they sell their house. They bring us a tin of mixed nuts at Christmas and visit us in the summertime when neighbors are all outside doing yard work. They love to tell people they are living in sin and then they chuckle as though they just let out a saucy secret.

In Box Four, lives a single woman with four little dogs. She is obsessed with her dogs and travels to many dog shows. Mrs. D is a Californian divorcee with expensive tastes. She has remodeled and decorated her home many times. The decor is large European style furniture, stuffy and uncomfortable looking. Her children never come to visit and I wonder if she is lonely.

In Box Five live our very best friends, Mr. and Mrs. G. Mr. G and my husband, Pete are garage and workshop buddies. Mr. G designed our new third car garage and helped Pete build the structure so he became a daily helper and part of the family. When Pete turned 70 last month, Mr. and Mrs. G came to the family birthday party in Anacortes. Mrs. G. is a schoolteacher who works all day with emotionally disturbed children at an elementary school in Sedro Woolley.

They are new grandparents and still have their family house in Lake Chelan. Once a month they cross Stevens Pass to spend time with their daughters and grandchild. We met the daughters when they came to visit last summer. When Mr. G had his second heart attack and Pete spent much time at the hospital with him while Mrs. G was working. Mrs. G reads my poems to her third grade class.

That brings me to the rental houses in my neighborhood - five boxes in all. Two young men in their 30s live in Box Six. One is a strong six foot burly man who helps Pete lift things that are too heavy for one person. He drives a milk truck and leaves at 4:00 am to start his deliveries. His cousin lives with him and both are hard-working people who mostly are not at home. Across the street from them is Box Seven where are favorite rental person has just moved to another location in Shelter Bay. He inherited a million dollars from a wealthy aunt so he purchased a 500,000 house on the slough with views of the boats and tugs going by. He still stops by to visit and has asked us to come down and try out his new hot tub and to meet his new California girlfriend. He loves to fish, go crabbing, and garden. In the summer he brings us freshly cooked crabs and vegetables from his garden. Last month he stopped by with a quart of fresh oyster stew. We consider him part of our family too.

The other three rental houses are rented by people we do not know. They all seem to keep to themselves. The newest renter is a blonde lady who runs a business out of her house. She charges 30 dollars an hour for an introductory massage. We see cars come and go. Guess we will have to try this service out just to see what really is going on. The other two rentals are at the end of the cul de sac out of our vision range. Both Pete and I are confessed window watchers and really care about our neighborhood. People come and go but their stories change with the times we live in.

The Newlyweds

I stumbled into my marriage like a newborn chick falling out of a nest. Ignorance and bliss described this fatal attraction. Had I used logic and reason, I would have paused and taken another five years to grow up. But as a teenager, I lived for the moment and perhaps thought this event would be a fast motion picture - a place where I could leave whenever I liked, being careful not to spill my popcorn on the way out.

Peter and I had met in high school at a Friday night canteen dance. He gave me a ride home in his 1934 Plymouth and we became fast friends ever after. We liked being a couple, a security that gave us a partner for the proms and football games. We looked like Mutt and Jeff, Pete was 6'2" and I was 5'1". Pete drove me to and from school and we became daily companions. So when we got married on February 21st, 1963, we were both committed to a lifetime relationship. Or so we thought!

I remember during the wedding vows at the University Presbyterian Church, how scared I was to pronounce those sacred vows. Only at a wedding ceremony do you make commitments so unrealistic. "For better or worse" - how bad will it get? I am thinking. "In sickness or health" - I hate being around sick people and taking care of a sick person wasn't going to work for me. "Till death do we part" - that sounds like forever. We will be old and decrepit together. This vow experience sounded like a recipe for disaster.

The planning of our wedding had gotten out of control. Pete's parents wanted a huge wedding with all the trimmings and offered financial support, so my parents gave in and we moved the wedding to the University Presbyterian Church which held the 200 guests that showed up. I not only felt like a newborn chick falling out of a nest but like a peewee clown at a circus full of strangers. I consoled myself with the fact that we were going to receive a lot of gifts. Who would deny 200 presents? Not me. In 1963, wedding presents were of a practical nature to help the couple furnish their new place. In our case a new place meant a small apartment at Bretz Manor in the Greenwood suburb of Seattle. Due to an abundance of presents, we received three toasters, three irons, three coffee pots, etc. etc. This newborn chick, me, would certainly be happy spending the rest of her life in the kitchen with all these new appliances. Wrong! I didn't even know how to cook! I tried my best but my dinners bordered on unhealthy and dangerous. One night I made spaghetti sauce from stratch like my mom and sister did. Sitting at our cheap dining table, we both struggled through the red goo sitting on a pile of mushy noodles. "Do you have any parmesan cheese for this?" Pete asked. Annoyed by his question and feeling guilty about my lack of cooking skills, I quietly reached across the table and dumped the whole spaghetti mess into his lap. He jumped up, grabbed his car keys, and took off. And so the spats of the newlyweds continued. I would slam cupboard doors and he would grab his car keys and leave. Our disagreements were never heated affairs. We both knew how to apologize, kiss, and makeup.

"For better or worse" - we had a lot of those events during our first five years of marriage. The worst events were Pete's accident at Todd Shipyard, the military assignment to the US Navy, and my parents' divorce.

The best events were The World Fair, dinners at the Space Needle, vacations in Hawaii, and a steady income for both of us. Our first child wasn't born until January 17, 1969 so we had plenty of time to grow up together - six whole years.

Going steady in high school was nothing like being married. I don't think living together gives a clue either. Adjustments and compromises must be continuous for a marriage to last as long as ours has. On February 21, 2013 we will have our 50th Wedding Anniversary. I asked my husband, "Why do you think we made it so long?" He smiled and said, "Our love and friendship." I replied, "Oh come-on, what really made things work?" With a twinkle in his eye, he said, "Patience!"

Nineteen Sixty-two Blues

As I write this story, I am age 63 and Pete is age 64. We have been married since February 21, 1963. So, obviously after the Attraction and Break-up (a separate story}, we found each other a year later in 1962, started dating again and soon were married. This time Diana knew what she wanted and she wanted to be married and yes, Pete looked like the best choice. Well, I have to be fair and tell how my year off from the relationship went but 1962 was such an ugly experience, I don't even want to write about it.

During 1962, my mother and father were fighting and talking about divorce. This was not a new experience for me, but the house-hold environment for my brothers and sisters was unhappy and tense. I, of course, was feeling guilty for leaving home and experiencing the wild oats of university life while my sibs were suffering. Finally my Mom left my Dad and moved to the University District into a large brick house on University Way. My sister Flora and three brothers lived with Lola, but Pam stayed at Les's house in Edmonds to pursue a nursing degree at Everett Community College. 1962 became a year of loneliness for Lola and a year of guilt for Diana. Double blues!

Although I visited with my mother I could not fix her problems. She was unhappy as a divorcee and her choice of boyfriends was not good. My three brothers were not doing well at school and became involved in drugs which were readily available in the 1960's, especially inside the city schools. While I was trying hard to enjoy my year of freedom from Peter and the new life as a college student, my experiences had been disappointing. I became disillusioned as to what career I wished to pursue. My grades slipped from B's to C's. I found it hard to make friends at such a large university. The professors were not as accessible as my teachers had been in high school. My only friend was a roommate, an Eskimo from Alaska, who attended medical school. She missed her family like I did. She had no boyfriends in her life. We often ate together in the kitchen at the boarding house where she shared her raw fish with me. Since she worked at the University of Washington Hospital, I decided to look for a job at the hospital too. With the divorce, my Mom was having money problems, and I knew I had to support myself as soon as possible.

I took a job at the University Hospital as a part-time autoclave worker. I cleaned surgical instruments in a large stainless steel sink and loaded the large autoclave oven. This was not a glamorous job but paid above minimum wage and I worked at night so I could attend school during the day. I was surviving but the excitement of being a Freshman at the U was turning into a school of hard knocks.

I often thought about Peter and how his life was going. We talked on the phone sometimes, and he tried to cheer me up but

I could tell that he was not happy either. His grades were slipping at Everett Community College and he was thinking of making a change. I too needed a change. I couldn't see paying for more classes when I no longer knew what career I wanted. I decided to pay a Career Counselor to find me a better paying job. She suggested I attend Petersen's Business School and train for keypunching. The computer industry was growing and computer jobs were readily available everywhere. After my business training, I took a full-time job at The Bon Marche downtown. Now I had money in my pockets and started to feel better about life. I even moved to a fancy apartment with a balcony in the Greenwood district and rode the city bus back and forth to work.

Peter dropped out of college also and started a Machinist Apprenticeship at Todd's Shipyard. The next time he called me, he asked me if I would consider dating again and I said yes. We both had money to spend and a sense of security with our careers. The dating this time was at a much higher level, because we could afford to take trips together, stay at fancy hotels, and eat at the best restaurants. We became engaged again and set a date for the wedding. This time we both knew what we wanted - each other but no family for at least seven years. After a large expensive wedding, which Pete's parents paid for, at the University Presbyterian Church, we honeymooned in Portland, Oregon. The early years of marriage were a continuation of our courtship.

Observation From Below

I feel so light and wiggly. My neck is almost strong enough to stay in one spot. My kicking legs never seem to stop except with I crash into a deep sleep and then I look like a bandit caught holding up a bank with my arms stretched far above my head. I am surrounded by the noise of chatter, jet-ski boats, windy pine trees, laughter and the smells of cooking. There is much I don't understand but I am in love with learning and looking and seem to be the focus of everyone's attention. What a happy way to be. I poop and I am changed, I cry when I'm hungry and am instantly fed to my satisfaction, and people love to rock me, hug me, and carry me around. My name is Samuel Pete Walker and I am 26 inches long and weigh fifteen pounds.

I am far away from home because I traveled eight hours yesterday in my car-seat. My mother, Susan Lynn, sat beside me in the backseat keeping a well-trained eye on my every move - but I hardly moved at all as I slept most of the way. My Dad is such a good driver that I felt safe as we climbed the steep Snoqualmie Pass, through the flat wheat lands of Moses Lake and Spokane, and on into Idaho and Montana reaching our final destiny at Flathead Lake. My great uncle Herman rented an old family house there for my first family reunion. I like lying here in the living room in a rocking davenport upon my blue and white baby blanket. I have a blue cotton tee and matching shorts that snap over my disposable diaper. My blue eyes match my outfit. When I am changed people coo and laugh and that makes me pee even more. My Mom even laughs and coos when I do the big yellow pasty job. But my grandma makes a wrinkly face with her nose held high in the air like she's not too impressed with my stinky smell.

I am trying to talk. I can say "Ah" and "Oh" and smiling and gurgling is easy too. I intensely watch the faces of the men and women who fuss over me to see if I can imitate them. So many people in one house - three great aunties, three great uncles, two great grandfathers, one great grandmother, two grandparents, and children ages ten to 24. They look down at me as they pass through the living room. The females ask to hold me and are surprised to find me so solid and stiff on my feet. The males are less relaxed with me and seem to stiffen up so I try to cooperate but the awkward positions they put me in feel strange to me, like they are afraid I might crack or break. An old man walks by and says he doesn't like babies so I hope he doesn't pick me up. When I get too tired of all the handling and people noises, my Mom puts me to sleep in the back bedroom, out of sight, to resume my bandit position for an hour or two.

My daily routine has been interrupted by this large gathering of the family. I find it hard to drink my bottle with so many distractions around me. Auntie Sharon is playing with my feet.

A line-up is taking place like at McDonalds to get a share of the baby bouncing act. My Grandfather Pete knows how to play with me and lies beside me on the floor. He waves his fingers above my head while I roll on my side for a closer look at the action. Rolling over is my latest trick. My Grandmother Diana carries me on her shoulder and walks proudly around the house. I feel high and mightly as on the roof-top. I love biting her shoulder too as I have hard gums that are trying to produce something unknown to me.

I could stay here forever, in this house by the lake, floating from lap to lap, basking in human attention from all these relatives who wish they were babies too. But after three days, my mother packs up my diaper bag, bottles, and stroller and back in the car seat I go. This time we will do a night time travel so I will miss the scenery and can sleep all the way. No one wants me to leave. I will grow too much until they see me again. But next year I will be able to talk and walk and look in all those cupboards that I couldn't open this time. I will swim in the lake too as my Mom has dipped my toes in and I like the feel of ice cold lake water. I didn't even cry. My Dad will take me for a boat ride and maybe on the jet-ski or on the kite-board. "Shhh", my mother says as she climbs into the truck. She has a pillow and looks tired and I get the look that says go to sleep so I can too.

The Occupiers

The Vancouver, BC, sky-train made the usual stop at Stadium Station. This day on November 22nd 2011, the train was full of holiday shoppers and the usual suburban riders. As the doors briskly slid open, a young man in his 20's entered. Pete and I moved back to make room. The stranger seemed agitated and started a conversation with us. "I got the call," he said. "My friends at Robson Square are being sprayed with tear gas." We immediately knew he was one of the occupiers of Vancouver in a hurry to get into the action.

Taking a closer look, we saw he had a gas mask in one hand and a backpack in the other. His Converse canvas laced up sneakers were moving back and forth as if he was willing the sky-train to move faster. He could have been a model for a painting I thought. His dress was a 1960's look, holey jeans and plaid green and black skirt hanging out loosely over his rugged slept-in jeans. His cheek bones were high and his large full lips hid under a Mark Twain mustache. Curly locks of dish-water blonde flowed downward almost to his waist. He reminded me of Johnny Dep in "The Pirates of the Caribbean." The pupils of his eyes were large and dark, hiding the true color of a blue or brown. His stance was 6 foot tall and his formidable demeanor announced a presence of integrity and purpose.

Pete and I were sympathetic to his cause and he sensed that we were on his side. He was a young person out to change the world. We felt like it was the 60's again- a time when Viet Nam protestors were the agitators of the downtown cities. We were grateful for the protestors of the 60's as President Nixon was impeached and the US Government became a force for the people once again. We are hoping the occupiers of all the cities will again change the goals of their governments. Afraid of the violence in the streets, we take on a calmer way of changing government. We regularly write our representatives and send e-mails with clear language that we demand change.

The sky-train lurched to a sudden stop at Granville Station. The occupier leaped from the train, ran to the escalators, and taking two steps at a time soon disappeared from our view. I had said, "Good luck to you," as he was leaving and Pete had said, "Be safe!" Although we were total strangers we had formed a bond in less than 3 minutes. A part of us wanted to go with him to Robson Square, but at our age of 70 we avoid the outdoor cold and the potential violent spots.

Premier Christy Clark of B.C. government said in the "Province Daily Newspaper," "citizens have had enough of the downtown occupiers. I think people are fed up with all this nonsense. It's not time for them to move. It's time for them to close up shop. I'm fed up with it." Emotions were high on both sides. The downtown stores were decorated for Christmas sales - Black Friday, the biggest sales day of the year was about to start. As we walked down Robson Avenue on the 22nd of November, we saw signs in front of the Art Museum and city park across the street that said "No tents allowed here." The eviction notice had gone into effect and the occupiers had moved to another public location, Robson Square Park. This was an area down by the waterfront and under bridges where the occupiers could stay dry. But, alas, this was not to be. Another eviction notice the next day caused them to search for a new place. The occupiers were so agitated that they marched through downtown carrying metal tent frames above their heads to make their point. Hundreds of occupiers blocked city intersections and a human chain lay down on the street to stop traffic. Eventually the police showed up and made arrests while occupiers shouted, "Let them go!! Let them go!!"

In the evening tucked snuggly in our hotel suite at the Sands Inn by the English Bay, we watched the evening CBC news. We saw the young man that we saw earlier on the sky-train. His snarled angry face was close to an armored policeman. He probably spent the night in the jail with others, I am thinking. I felt happy for him, he was making an important statement against his government that was no longer listening to the people. Time to get out my angry pen and write more protest letters to my congressmen. I go to sleep thinking about the brave occupiers who are not afraid to disrupt the status quo.

Opposites

As I sat in the uncomfortable plastic chair by my sister's bedside in the intensive care wing at Mt. Vernon Hospital I was afraid and worried, more for myself than for my sister because I did not wish to lose her. We were like identical twins, sidekicks, but very much opposite personalities. Every day that I took a breath, I was aware that Pam was living close by in Anacortes. She watched over me and I watched over her, from a distance of course, but I always knew she was there and would come at a moment's notice if I needed her and visa-versa. Sisters are like that - even opposites.

Pam and I grew up in the same household, same parents, and same siblings. I was the first-born and she was born three years later. I was the straight-laced serious child and she the happy-go-lucky child. My parents as they produced more children required much help from Pam and me. But Pam seemed to sneak out of most of the chores and I just picked up the pace and did double duty. At school I was expected to get all A's on my report card. After all I was the brightest child and was constantly told not to waste my talents. Pam's report card was filled with mostly C's and D's and my parents felt relieved that she had passed her classes and could move on to the next grade. She was the July child, always behind in school; I was the November child and always ahead in school.

Around our house, growing up together, I loved to do the cleaning and organizing chores like ironing, making beds, folding clothes and picking up the scattered toys. Pam enjoyed making a mess and spent much time in the kitchen cooking with Mother, baking cookies, decorating cookies, making spaghetti sauce,etc. She loved to make a mess and seemed to disappear when Lola cried out, "Okay, everybody, it's time for clean-up." Pam and I both liked the outdoors, we did share that trait. But Pam was athletic and could ski, swim, climb trees, and out-hike most boys. I almost flunked every PE class because I had no eye-hand coordination. Pam was the first to be picked for the team, me the last. She would sleep outside in the yard under the stars or inside a tent. I would snuggle in my freshly made bed and cuddle with my cat. No dirty messy outside for me.

Being close-knit sisters, we liked going places together. In the summer of 1985, Pam called me to invite me on a trip. We were older now, living in different states. I was still married and Pam had suffered a nasty divorce. She was now living in Montana, working as an emergency nurse at a hospital in Kalispell. Yes, she still liked a mess - bloody dead bodies and all. "Let' s go camping together for a week," she had said on the phone, "I just bought a new Ford truck with a sleeper on the back. I would like to drive the Canadian highway and stay at the state parks. We would have fun. Can you do it?"

My inner voice revolted at the word "camping" but I missed my sister so I said yes and we started making plans. I flew into Kalispell on a sunny July morning and Pam picked me up at the airport in her new Ford "Silver Bullet," a name that would live up to its' expectations. She had the back canopy all packed with her favorite camping equipment and a roll up mattress for us to share for our sleeping bags. We quickly headed out down a lesser traveled mountain road, traveling north to Canada. 1960s tunes were blaring from the new stereo radio and we were speeding along. Soon a state patrolman passed us going the opposite direction. Pam hit the brake, slowed down, looked in her rear mirror and said, "Oh shit! He turned around." Pulling off the road due to a loud siren, Pam shuffled through the glove locker to find the necessary papers. "Let me do the talking," she said. Looking up at the officer, she flashed her nurse's card and said, "I'm sorry, but I forgot I wasn't on an emergency medical run." The officer wasn't buying her story, probably due to all the camping gear in the back. "Even nurses have to obey the speed limit," he said and wrote up a costly speeding ticket. As we pulled away, she said, "What a jerk. Diana, since we agreed to split all the costs of this trip, half this ticket is yours." "Nice try," I said, but I wasn't the one speeding, so this one is yours." We started laughing, the music came on, and Pam kept the truck up to speed but not over the limit. Once in Canada, we started looking for a state park.

We had a great time in the Provincial Park, swimming in the lake, roasting hotdogs over the open fire and visiting in lawn chairs by the "Silver Bullet." However, sleeping in the truck that night brought us no fun and no sleep. In the spot next to us a group of college boys, enjoying Spring Break, had set up camp with several tents. As they nurtured a keg of beer throughout the night, their voices became louder and louder. At two in the morning, Pam said to me, "Are you sleeping."

"No I am not; those drunken kids are driving me crazy." "Okay, I've had it!" said Pam, and off she went to the camp next doors, her long flannel flowered night gown whipping in the breeze. I don't remember what she said but I know it had absolutely no effect on the boys. Soon we were packing up our gear and on the road at four in the morning. She woke up the ranger at the station on our way out and told him about the disorderly boys. The ranger was still in his pajamas but promised to take care of the matter in the morning. The next day was a strain on our relationship. Two tired sisters out to find another camp ground. By the time we got to Sidney, B.C. we were staying in motels.

The cardiologist was speaking to Pam so I stopped my daydreaming to listen to his remarks. "I would like to do an angiogram to see what is causing your chest pain." I followed the gurney down to the surgery room, explaining that I was her sister and would stay in the waiting room until the procedure was over. It was six o'clock on a sunny August day in 2012. I waited by myself for two hours until a small petite Asian man caught my eye. "Are you Pam's sister," he asked. "Yes, I said." "She had a heart attack and we had to put in two stints. We will take her to her room soon but we need to monitor her heart for the next three days." I stayed with her off and on for the next few days because that's what sisters do - even opposites.

The Peace Maker

"Diana, check on your brothers," my mother yelled from the kitchen. We both heard the ruckus from the back bedroom and the cries- "It's mine. I had it first!" Lola was feeding baby brother Herman John and couldn't leave the kitchen. Down the hallway I stomped. As I peered from the doorway, Mark hollered, "Run, Lester, Run! She's got the spatula!" And so they did, in opposite directions of course. I was faster, and scooped them up, sat them down in separate bedrooms and said, "Time-out for ten minutes or else, waving the spatula in the air. I was the second mother in those days. Little did I know that conflict management would be a much needed skill to my later careers as a teacher and high school principal.

I did not grow up in a quiet environment. My house was filled with the noise of too many children· and uncontrolled chaos. We, all eight of us, lived in a small three bedroom rambler with one bathroom in a multiple unit project, called "Rolling Meadows" - nothing was rolling and there certainly were no meadows, just flat land, no trees, dust in the air in the summer, and snow drifts in the winter. The desolate place was Rapid City, South Dakota. The neighborhood children gravitated to our yard because that was the action spot- outdoor games of hide and seek, tag, and cops and robbers took over the yards of the look-alike houses. Lola's kitchen was the hang-out for the housewives who filled their cups with the ever-present Folgers and smoked the endless Lucky Strikes and Virginia Slims. And, of course, I was the responsible baby sitter keeping an eye on various children that came and went from our front doors. I never really thought about whether I liked this job or not. I just did it.

The thump of his work boots was loud on the stairs. He yelled, "Who the hell is in charge of this school!" My Secretary Marian's face said it all. With a frown she reached for the phone and dialed the Renton School District security department. Mr. Janicky swaggered through Marian's office and into mine. Then he stopped abruptly as he saw his opponent was only five foot one inches, blonde, female, and wearing a black tailored suit. Leaning towards me, he said, "I am really pissed!" "Please sit down, Mr. Janicky. "You have a right to be angry. Your daughter has been a challenge to you and to our school. Let's talk about how we can help her and improve things for the future. I saw the large man's shoulders sag, as he lowered himself into the chair opposite my desk. The smell of alcohol pierced the musty room. "I have a plan for Jennifer, but I need your help," and so I began soothing the fears of a tired old man.

His daughter, Jennifer, had moved in with him two years ago when his ex wife had died from an overdose of drugs. Neither Mr. Janicky nor Jennifer liked this new arrangement. Rebelling, Jennifer had been kicked-out of the local high school and had entered our school as a new student. She quickly hooked up with the drug users in our building, attending the 1980 neighborhood after-school drug and sex parties. Also, she was six-months pregnant which really ticked her Dad off. Last week a teacher had caught her smoking a joint in the bathroom so I had suspended her for one week.

"But you know how it is," said Mr. Janicky. "I work forty hours a week at Boeing and over-time on the week-ends. Most of the time I don't know where she is. School is the safest place for her to be. I said firmly," I won't let Jennifer back into school until she enrolls in the YWCA teen-parent program and the NA program at the Renton Area Youth Services. If she doesn't do this, she will continue to live on the street and probably end up in jail. He was now listening.

Peter Norman Caple (02-12-1942,BD)

The year was 1947. The red-haired five year-old grasped his Mom's hand tightly. The lights of New York harbor were all aglow; people on the shores waved American flags to welcome the new immigrants. Peter looked up at his new father, dressed neatly in his crisp Coast Guard uniform. Peter was very fond of his new father as he had never known his birth father, who had disappeared during World War II, shortly after he was born. Myrtle, Peter's Mom was dressed in her finest silk dress and high heels. Such a gorgeous red-haired beauty she was and she had given up her English homeland to start a new dream with the man she loved.

Peter, dressed in his blue English suit, pulled his wool cap down over his ears. The air smelt damp and sooty but the smells were not as pungent as the sooty bombs of World War II. During the London Blitz of 1943, Peter and his Mom had spent many a night hiding underground in the air raid shelters. Looking up, Peter saw another mother-figure rising out of the harbor with a torch above her head. Myrtle said to her son, "Look, Peter, the Statute of Liberty, the magical omen of peace and freedom." The son nodded as if he understood her every word but seeing his mother happy was all that mattered to him.

Hoyt Jack Caple knew adjusting to America would be a huge step for his new wife and soon to be adopted son. Hoyt's mother Cora was waiting for them in the small village town of LaConner, Washington with a room upstairs all fixed up for her new grandson whom she had yet to meet. But first, Jack, as he was affectionately called by Myrtle, wished to show off his country to his new son and wife. They traveled slowly from the East Coast to the West Coast, stopping at all the National Parks along the way. Peter does not remember the details of this travel or his two years in LaConner where he attended kindergarten and first grade. But Cora's house still stands on Second Street, across from the Nell Thorn Restaurant. Cora's house is now remodeled and occupied by another family. Jack Caple was still in the Coast Guard after the war and was assigned to the Seattle station.

As a young man in his 20's, Jack had joined the Coast Guard in LaConner, which had been located where the Calico Cubboard in now. His job was to help the local police catch the rum runners as they swiftly navigated through the Swinomish Slew. Prior to World War II, Jack was stationed at various locations in the South, including Virginia and Mississippi. During the war Jack rose to the rank of Commander and was on a ship at the battle of Normandy, where unfortunately he lost much of his hearing. Jack and Myrtle later met in London at the end of the war and fell in love. Upon returning to the states, Jack was stationed at Norfolk, Virginia for a few years. His Coast Guard training included ship inspection which became a lucrative occupation for him after his retirement from the Coast Guard.

Peter attended grade school in Norfolk, but remembers very little of this time. He does remember the children calling him "turnip top" but his mother told him this was really "carrot-top" but because there were no fresh carrots in England during the war, Peter always said turnip instead of carrot. The English language was not hard for Peter to adopt, but his mother always had the English accent even into her later years.

Peter attended junior high school in Lynnwood, Washington His father was now stationed in Seattle and still doing ship inspections for the Coast Guard. Myrtle and Jack had purchased an old country cottage in Meadowdale on five acres. Myrtle raised chickens, lambs, and goats like she had done in England. Peter drank goat's milk and ate rice pudding and roast lamb. His diet was very English at home but very American at school and his favorite hang out was the A & W Root beer stand where the waitresses rode around on roller skates to deliver cheeseburgers and fries on trays to rolled down windows. Pete's favorite subjects at school were auto shop, machine shop, wood-working, and football. Paper, pen and books were a struggle for him as he was dyslexic. During the 40's and 50's there were no special classes for learning disabilities. Pete's teachers loved his eager smile, polite character, and his father was the President of the school board which didn't hurt either. So Peter's teachers happily passed him on from grade to grade with a card full of C's, except, of course, his shop teachers who gave him all A's.

At age fifteen, Peter had his first job at Ferrill's Auto Wrecking Yard in Lynnwood. He knew all about car parts from his collection of Hot Rod magazines. He could build an engine and take one apart. Spending more time at work and less time at school, he eventually earned a car of his own. Ferrill let Pete pick out any old car he wanted from the wrecking yard so Pete picked out a 1947 Ford Convertible, burgundy color, with a Surefit white cloth top, flathead V-8 engine, three carburetors and a¾ cam. Ferrill hauled the old ford without an engine to Pete's driveway much to his folk's displeasure and surprise. Out went Jack's new pink Cadillac and Myrtle's old Buick while Pete's new project took over the double car garage. Heated discussions took place between Pete's parents but, wishing to keep their restless teenager busy, the automobile project won out. Pete rebuilt the Ford from the ground up, including the V-8 engine. Ferrill supplied all the materials and Jack helped his son with the smaller projects but Pete did the difficult remodel which took nine months to complete, just in time for his 16th birthday.

While attending (and I use this word loosely) Edmonds Senior High School, Pete rebuilt a second car, a 1934 Plymouth. This was a 6 cylinder engine, three carburetors, lowered with 14 inch wheels, trunk was leaded-in, with a telephone in the back seat, burgundy color, and a black shrunken plastic head hung from the rear-view mirror. Diana had the pleasure of meeting Pete at a Friday night Canteen dance and received a ride home that night in the 1934 Plymouth. (For more stories about Peter, please read Diana's other stories, starting with "The Attraction.")

Peter and Jay

The awkward shy tall man approached the podium. Shuffling his feet he gazed across the audience of 200 people at the Shelter Bay Community Center. His bifocals slipped forward as he bent a silver-gray head toward a carefully scripted computer generated text. He usually wore blue jeans and white New Balance tennis shoes but not today. Looking clean cut and formal, he wore tailored black slacks with gray stripes, shiny black polished shoes and a pull over blue sweater matching slate-blue eyes. Even though public speaking was not a favorite genre, his demeanor was full of joy and pride. Gretchen had asked him to speak at her mother's funeral service. Peter had replied quickly, "Yes, I would be happy to do so."

Wife Diana and daughters, Susan and Sharon, .sat in the front row; cheeks smeared with teary running makeup and shredded Kleenex wadded in their hands. The room smelt of catered food, a mix of shrimp, cucumber sandwiches, fruit salad and freshly made coffee. The daughters had not known their father was going to speak and knew their Dad could be too emotional sometimes. They gave their mother a worrisome look and she whispered, "It's okay, he has been practicing all week."

Of those gathered for Jay Campbell's memorial, fifty were relatives from California, Oregon, and Washington. The oldest son, Ty, spoke first, followed by nieces, nephews, grandchildren and friends from Shelter Bay. A constant theme emerged from each speech - "I always knew I was her favorite!" Jay had the penetrating eye contact of an encouraging listener and after a short visit with her, you felt uplifted and glad you had wandered into her parlor for a brief session. Peter always felt special and was nicknamed "Petie." He had painted her house one summer and loved every minute of it. Jay would stand under the ladder with fresh cookies and water for her favorite handyman. He shoveled her driveway when it snowed, and replaced her garage door twice when she ran into it with her sedan.

Pete was the last to speak and there seemed to be nothing left to say, but we were all surprised by his neighborhood stories about Jay. The favorite story about the skunk made everyone laugh. Jay had been a naturalist and loved living among the animals. Many raccoons had made a home under her porch. The deer always walked through her yard, reaching up to bite the fresh apples and rose buds from her Martha Washington prize rose bush. And, yes, one day a friendly skunk camped out under Jay's porch. Jay played her favorite opera music (sometimes too loudly for her neighbors). She claimed the music soothed the skunk and kept the noxious odor at bay. I think Jay had lost her sense of smell by this time, as a visit on the front porch always included a faint odor from under the porch.

After finishing his Jay stories, Peter paused and looked across the room at the Shelter Bay village, who had taken care of one of their own. "You know who you are, "he said, "too many people to mention by name. A big thank you to all of you who helped Jay stay in her home."

A Pocket Full of Fear

There is such a thing, a moment in time that changes a person forever. Some people call this a "wake-up call." On September 21st, 1987, I had such a moment. Until this day my office in my school building was my safe haven. As a Re-Entry Co-ordinator for the Renton School District, I recruited and placed high school dropouts back into the system, usually within the classes at my own Alternative High School. So, through my doors walked a variety of human salvage - the drug dealers, addicts, teen parents, juveniles on probation, and the highly intelligent and gifted types who dropped out of the mundane school system due to boredom. I truly loved these eccentric, non-establishment teens and did my best to convince them to return to school for a diploma or GED.

In the 1970's this troubled population of teens were mild mannered and easy to counsel. But through each passing year, the teens became bolder, more street wise, and less likely to return to school. By the 1980's, gangster rap, MTV, lucrative street crime, and available weapons became a problem for all the schools. In 1985, the Renton School District started adding policemen to their buildings and video cameras to hallways and parking lots. The occasional gun incident was reported and our building adopted the practice of lock-down procedures.

In 1987, September, as usual, was my heaviest volume of appointments for student placement. Sometimes I would have "walk-ins" to accommodate. On September 21st, two gangster looking black men walked into my office. The older man was dressed in low-slung baggy jeans, red sweatshirt, and wore a plastic shower cap pulled down over his ears. The younger boy wore similar gang garb, but looked more innocent with his calm, intelligent doe-ful eyes. I recognized the garb as the California Bloods. Mr. Shower-cap-man said to me, "I'm here to enroll my home-boy in your school." Mr. Homeboy seemed intimidated by his sidekick and gave me a look that said, "This could get dangerous."

Now I was feeling intimidated, my neck hairs were sizzling, my hands felt sweaty and cold, and my heart was pounding out of my chest. My logical brain, always good in an emergency, was assessing the situation. My nervousness was well disguised, but something else was going on; my sixth sense was noticing that Mr. Plastic-shower-cap-man had his hand in his pocket wrapped around a concealed object. He repeated, "I want my homeboy enrolled in your school today." I knew by his cold steel bullet eyes that he had a gun in his pocket and probably would draw it if necessary. He was used to getting his own way.

Somewhere from outside myself, I heard my own voice say, "Certainly, Sir. Would next Monday be a good day for your friend to start school?" I quickly filled out an enrollment card, keeping my questions to a minimum. I handed Mr. Homeboy my business card with the date and time to show up for school and suggested he bring a notebook, paper and pen for first day orientation. "Welcome to our school," my sixth sense said in a hollow tone that didn't sound like myself at all. Quietly they left my office without a single question.

The backs of my legs pulled my body straight down into my chair, my body was dead weight, and I felt so relieved I knew I could wet my pants and not even care. Marian, my elderly white haired secretary came running in and said, "Oh, dear, those were the worst kids I have yet to see. Are you okay?" Not to add further to an already bad situation, I lied, "Everything's OK, Marian," But, I knew in my bones that I had been lucky and this "wake-up call" was not without a purpose. I needed to ratchet-up the safety and security of my office and the classrooms. I didn't want this incident to happen to one of my teachers or my secretary.

The next day I looked at safety options by visiting a store that specialized in home alarm systems. I discovered a nifty little item called a body alarm, a two inch square metal object that clips onto a belt or pocket. The button in the middle when pressed sets off a large piercing wail much like a fire alarm. I bought one for myself and one for each staff person in my building. I might not be any safer in the future but at least I could signal for help.

The Reluctant Visitor

The doorbell was ringing and I was dreading this encounter with the person on the other side of the door. Pam, my look-alike sister, was waiting and wondering what was so important that I had asked her the night before to please show up for a discussion of an urgent medical problem. I knew I could not discuss the problem over the phone for several reasons. I would probably break down and cry. Pam is hard of hearing and wears hearing aids so she misses a lot of conversation over the phone. Pete and I had already visited the Skagit Valley cancer clinics and wished to show her the pamphlets and discuss our options with her. Pam is a home health care visiting nurse for the Island Hospital in Anacortes, Washington. She has worked as a surgical assistant, a hospital nurse, and a hospice nurse. After much experience there is not too much stuff she has not dealt with, however she is terrible about handling medical emergencies in her own family. One time she took her son to the emergency room and left him outside in the car, forgetting for a moment where he was. I am worried about how she will react to our bad news.

At this point we had not told anyone in the family about Peter's prostate cancer - not even our two daughters. We were still in the denial and shock phase and basically searching for a miracle. We decided to consult Pam because she was very close family and knew most of the doctors in Skagit Valley and could help us with our medical decisions. Being the older sister, I hated to jolt her with bad news - I was the protective one and often helped her with her emotional baggage. As I opened the door and looked into her face, her eyes had the worried look, her mouth a frown, and her sagging shoulders had the "I would like to go home look." Looking at my Sister Pam is like looking in the mirror. When we travel together, people mistake us for twins. When she visits her clients in Shelter Bay, she has to say, "I am Diana's sister, Pam. I am not Diana."

Peter and I invite Pam to sit at the dining room table and pour her a cup of tea. She knows what is coming as we have prostate cancer information spread across the table. We had done our home work, consultations with the Oncologist, the Radiologist and the Surgeon. Now we were saturated with too much information and still no positive solutions. Pam's first question was, "Have you had biopsies done?" Pete said, "Yes, Dr. Cornelius has taken seven biopsies, and the results were all seven showed Stage Four Cancer." Stage four is mid-range and must be treated either surgically or with radiation. Both procedures had equal risks of incontinence and impotency. Pam had her "nurse's hat" on and started looking at Pete's medical reports. Dr. Cornelius had given us colorful graphics that showed the biological placement of the prostate gland inside the body and multi-colored blobs that showed the stages of cancer from the beginning to the end. Stage eight was the worst stage where the cancer has spread to other organs and the bones. Pete's mid-line stage was still treatable but more biopsies were needed around the prostate area so Dr. Cornelius wished to not only remove the totally involved prostate gland but do more biopsies to further insure the cancer was not spreading to other organs. This is the kind of information that keeps one from sleeping at night. Actually, I felt like I hadn't slept in weeks. Looking my friends in the eyes and saying, "I'm fine," was wearing me down. I certainly was not fine and neither was Peter.

Now that Pam was on board with us, I was feeling somewhat better until she said, "What a bad deal this is! This will be a tough decision for you to make, but based on my experience, I would take Dr. Cornelius' advice and have the prostate gland removed. Stage Four Cancer is aggressive and can return and move into other organs. He is absolutely right about this. Radiation is tricky because the radiation may not stop aggressive cancer. Radiation is best used at the beginning cancer stages." We are listening carefully to her advice and since we liked Dr. Cornelius we were leaning towards his recommendation for surgery. Pam had confirmed what we were already thinking.

I have always loved my Sister Pam and will forever and ever but at this particular moment I gained a respect for her professional side that I had never realized before. She is a great nurse and made us feel like the solution was do-able and the risks not so great. She talked to us about the solutions to impotency and incontinence.

She said she would be at Island Hospital with us and help with Pete's recovery if we needed anything. Suddenly we had someone on our side and the journey ahead seemed bearable. Later that day we called our friends and neighbors and spread the news about Pete's pending surgery. The more people we told the better we felt.

Eventually we sat down with each daughter and, although they had tears, they wished to be at the hospital with us and help with their Dad's recovery.

The final chapter to this story is that Peter's surgery on November 28th, 2005, was successful and all cancer was removed. All biopsies on the side organs were normal and future PSA blood samples were normal. Peter and I both feel we dodged a bullet and now are more sympathetic to others who venture down the cancer road. We now volunteer as support persons for others who face the difficult journey of decision making.

The Risk Factor

There comes a time in everyone's life when one has to break from the mold and jump into the unknown. After five years as Manager of the Re-Entry Program at RVTC, I had a comfortable daily routine. Mostly I served as a counselor to the teachers and the students, following the at-risk students from entry to exit. As the reputation of our success with the student drop-out population grew, so did our little school. The waiting list grew to thirty plus students and we were able to fill the vacancies on a year-round basis. The Renton Community and parents were supportive of the program. It was most satisfying watching distraught students, labeled losers, turning their lives around, graduating with a high school diploma or GED.

I should have sensed the problem coming, but my boss, Dr. Delight handled the administrative and financial decisions for the Learning Center, so I was left out of the big picture. Dr. Delight managed many different programs at RVTC, such as ESL, Adult Basic ED, and other classes that came and went depending on the grant monies available. One day at a staff meeting, she announced that Olympia would end the funding for our Re-Entry Program and we would probably be moved off the college campus and into a public school as part of the Renton Public School System. I was stunned.

I had poured my heart and soul into building the Re-Entry Program and was frightened by this announcement. Who would manage the program once we moved off campus? Would our older students in their 20's be comfortable showing up to a public school building? Which high school principal would be chosen to take over this population? I didn't feel that any of the Renton School District administrators were right for the job. Many did not understand the fragile state of the drop-out student and still followed the old rules of suspension and conformity. What a risk this would be to me and my program.

Dr. Delight and I had many long talks about how all this change could be implemented. Nothing would change for the teachers as they already worked for RSD and were members o the teachers' union. It seemed I was the problem. Dr. Delight suggested we meet with the RSD Personnel Director to work on my job description and persuade RSD to hire me as a principal. What a dilemma for me; I hated the word principal. Our whole program was different from RSD's programs and I didn't want to follow school district policies or rules. I loved my job just as it was and especially being part of the college. The risk of moving me and my program under a public school umbrella was not what I wanted.

As the months passed by, I had to set aside my emotions and learn how to be a district team player. The risk of not cooperating could destroy everything I had built. Watching my boss , Dr. Delight, through the years attack problems head on and win her battles, I decided to shoulder my armor and go into the meetings with a hard-nosed determination. "Think like a man," Dr. Delight often said to me. There was no male principal in the Renton School District in the 1980's, but maybe I could be the first female. Maybe I could break through the glass ceiling, demand my just desserts, and become a team player.

Dr. Delight had a lot of clout with the RSD Superintendent so I began thinking in terms of strategies. After all, I had earned a principal's credential in the 70's while completing my Master's

Degree in Special Education. "Stand up for yourself and be a man," the voice inside my head proclaimed. Don't be afraid of change. I was already a manager with my own secretary, I could take the risk. Many of my daily tasks were similar to a principal's job, managing the teachers and troubleshooting the various human conflicts that happened within the program between teacher and student, student and student, and defusing anger between parents and the Learning Center. The increase in pay would be a plus. But I would have to work for a superintendent who had the power to hire or fire me on an annual basis. That was a risk I didn't like, as we had not seen eye to eye on many issues regarding the dropout students.

Eventually logic conquered fear, and I demanded an administrative job since that was what I had been doing for the last five years. The program had paid for itself at 300,000 dollars a year. The district could still have a salvage operation for the drop-outs. I knew I was more an asset than a liability. Dr. Delight and Dr.Roberts would help me make the transition. Excitement replaced fear. Opportunity was knocking loudly and I better step up to the plate.

The Road Less Traveled (Early Childhood)

Throughout my lifetime I gravitated to the road less traveled. At an early age, before five years old, I knew that I was different from the norm. Also, I was a constant observer and curious about all things in my environment. I was born November 28, 1942, during World War II. People were trying to survive after the Great Depression of 1929 and many families had gathered together to live in one house and share financial responsibilities. Many of my relatives lived in the spacious three story gray stucco house two blocks from St. Cloud Teachers' University. This three story house had an upstairs full of bedrooms and one bath. There was a servants quarters on one side of the house where my mom, dad, and I lived. The other bedrooms held my cousins, aunts and uncles. The kitchen, smelling like apple pies and pickling brine - always contained the aroma of homemade morsels. A musty attic and a large dark basement became play rooms for the children. My grandfather, John Cochrane, taught history at the university. Although we were poor, we were rich with literary language and lots of books. These were the days of gathering around the fireplace to hear the elders visit with each other while the children sat quietly, respectfully tuned into the web and flow of elder talk. We usually had our pajamas on and we knew if we behaved in a proper adult manner, we could stay up later. I particularly enjoyed Grandfather's literary voice as he read from Shakespeare, Milton and all the great writers of his time. He had a booming oratory manner, pronouncing difficult diction with a frown or a sneer. Sometimes the text was funny and we laughed until our tummies hurt. My grandfather taught me to read and write before school age so I skipped kindergarten and started first grade at the age of five.

From 1941 to 1945, most men were away from their families to serve in World War II. These young men of the country were drafted into the Army or other services. My Dad was drafted into the Air Force because he had mechanical knowledge of aircraft. During his time of service he rarely came home so he really had no time to spend with his first born child. In 1944 after the war he immediately enrolled in the local university to obtain a teaching certificate, paid for by the GI Bill. We were still living at grandfather's house. My mother was expecting a second child in 1944 but this was a tragedy in the making. The baby boy only lived one month due to an undeveloped lung. I don't remember much about my mom during this tragedy but I suspect she spiraled into a deep depression. My grandfather had the dominate influence on me these first five years and I realize that my love for rich literary language came from him and perhaps, genetically from Grandma Cochrane.

My grandmother, Lola Francis Gromley, married my grandfather John Carl Cochrane in the 1920s. I have vague uncomfortable memories about Grandma Cochrane as she had a "mental condition." As a young child she had grown up in an upper class society with servants. She loved literature and the arts and eventually became an elementary teacher. At college she studied languages, graduating with a Master's Degree in Latin. When she met my grandfather in her twenties, she had to give up her profession to be a wife and mother. Only single men and women were allowed to teach children. I suspect this was a difficult and unfair decision for her to make because she had an intellectually brilliant mind. Also, she grew up in a household of servants and knew nothing about how to keep house or raise children. My grandfather hired both a cook and a daily house-keeper to manage the house. He was off to the college each day and she was home alone with her five children and two servants. In the 40s during the war, when her children and grandchildren moved into her house, she had a lot of company and intellectual companionship. But even then, she had moods of sadness. I don't have fond memories of Grandmother Lola and was a bit frightened by her. Her mood swings were unpredictable and she had "fainting spells". In the dining room on the sideboard sat a silver dish containing sugar cubes. I was trained as a young child to give Grandmother Lola a sugar cube if she passed out. But because of all the available adults around, I don't remember giving her a sugar cube. Later in life, while in her 40s, her mind began to wander. My grandfather could no longer care for her and she was placed into a sanitarium. By the time I was a teenager, no-one talked about Grandma Lola. She had just disappeared into the sad recesses of her mind. Later in life, after she died, we figured out that her spells were caused by undiagnosed diabetes. Her son Bill and daughter Flora were diagnosed with diabetes.

Today we know that the lack of insulin does indeed affect the brain. My cousin Carol was diagnosed with diabetes, type two, three years ago. Everyone in my family has a glucose test once a year.

Rock-hopping

My stomach, chest, and arms tightly hug the earth beneath me. My legs are spread as far apart as I can manage. My left hand, fingers spread apart, digs deep into the arid sandy soil. I can feel the sand beneath my finger nails and I pray that my spread eagle position will keep me from sliding further into the abyss. I lay silently ten feet from the drop off that will take my body down

300 feet to the canyon bottom. I dare not continue to slide so I am frozen in time and space. My brain is lost inside the unused cellular spot - the spot reserved for rescue and emergency survival.

I remember when I was a child, growing up in the snowy hills of Northern Minnesota. Winter temperatures often hovered below freezing. My mother Lola had taught me how to survive in the snow when the upper crust was frozen into sheer ice. We often used cardboard boxes for sleds and propelled downward at amazing speeds. But occasionally the cardboard would give way and toss me out onto the slippery surface and I would start to spin and slide on my belly or back.

Mother showed me how to spread eagle on the icy snowy slopes and I knew how to stop my body instantly and then inch myself out of danger into a safe location, away from the other sliders and broken trees. This actually was a fun experience in my childhood days.

But, right now at this moment I am not having fun. I am afraid to move lest my body starts the downward slide again. I am glad my fellow hiking friends are able to seek safety from my fall. They can only watch in horror at my dilemma. Their silence rings loud inside the canyon walls. Here I am, clearly out of my comfort zone, not knowing if a spread eagle will work on this steep rocky shale in the southwestern desert. Yet I stay frozen against the soil and pray for the insight I need to survive.

Early morning at 5:00 am our group of rock hoppers gathered for a fun morning of exploration in the Rincon Mountains outside of Tucson, Arizona. We had parked our cars at the top of the mountain at the ranger's station and left another group of cars at the bottom of the saddle at the trail head. Our goal was to rock hop up the boulders, one rock at a time, until we reached the top. By noon our adventure would be over, as temperatures in the 90's were predicted and afternoon sunshine would not be pleasant for rock-hopping. Also, the rattle snakes would climb out of their holes to sunbath and hunt- not a safe place to be in the boulders.

My seasoned rock hopping friend, a 75 year old retired ranger, had taught me rock-hopping skills and I was a regular hiker with the Southern Arizona Hiking Club. "Diana," he said, "the trick to climbing over rocks is to pick out the most stable looking rock and just go for it - act in charge - simple as climbing up a ladder." He also carried a walkie-talkie that had a direct line to the ranger station so if someone fell, he could get medical help which usually meant a helicopter ride to Tucson Medical Center. I had much confidence in my hiking experience and observed the safety rules, but also knew that accidents could happen. But I didn't want to be the accident. I cleared the idea of broken bones out of my thinking. "Keep your spread eagle and take a deep breath - think, think, and think."

I slowly glanced behind and below to see if there was anything, a tree, rock, or bush, that might catch me if I started to slide downward again. Nothing! Just ten feet of sand between me and the drop off, into a 300 foot canyon. The same canyon I had safely climbed up earlier. Next, I glanced to my right and saw Sarah, who starting to fall with me had leapt to safety, aided by the other hikers who were able to grab her. We had all underestimated the slipperiness of the aspen leaves gathered on this slope. The two leaders ahead of us had no trouble with the crossing so like mindless sheep we had followed after them. Looking to my right I saw nothing to grab onto but the sandy soil which I still had my right hand buried into like a shovel at the beach. On my left, I spied a hopeful lower limb of a desert bush but this was two feet away which meant I would have to move sideways. I was afraid to leave the safety of my spread eagle.

Amazingly I developed a calm demeanor; I needed to muster courage and quick action to save myself. I continued to use my imagination to fool my body into hugging the ground. I pretended to be a large spider with a flat medicine ball for my center. I knew I had to throw my left boot towards the lower branch of the nearby bush. At the same moment I needed to slide my center weight to the left, keeping my arms spread, fingers dug into the dirt and my right leg at a 90 degree angle. Just like on the crusty snow in Minnesota. I knew I could do this. I also knew I had only one chance to make this happen. Quickly I lunged sideways and the small desert bush anchored in the rock held my left boot - never mind the pain of the cacti needle stuck into my leg. Again I repeated the same leftward lunge and now I had the cactus bush between my legs. Moving upward I could now reach a lower branch of the aspen tree and eventually pulled myself upright, hugging the tree for dear life. I continued moving sideways to the left, always hanging on to a branch until I reached the safety of the switchback trail.

Soon our group was hiking on flat land heading back to our cars. "I was so frightened for you," Sarah said, "that could have been me." I knew that I had truly escaped a brush with death. I decided never to rock-hop again and I never did and I never will.

Rocky Roads

We were a family of eight and fit perfectly into the large blue station wagon my folks loved to drive. In 1952 our station wagon was state of the art with two ashtrays up front and one on each side in the back. All windows were roll downs, the radio sometimes worked, and the heater ran too hot - no air conditioning and no seat belts. We were free to bounce around the car and over the seats while my Dad drove up front with the window open and a cig in his mouth. No trash bags were necessary because everything went out the window.

Sunday afternoon was the favorite time for a country ride and we loved to climb into the Big Blue. Mom and Dad rode up front, Diana (that's me), Pam and Flora Ann (ages 13, 10 and 8) rode on the back seat. I always got a window seat because I tended to get carsick. In the back of the wagon my Mother placed pillows, a sleeping bag, picnic food, extra clothes, and toys. This was where Mark, Herman, and Lester (ages 6, 4, and 2) and our golden retriever Zip hung out and the three brothers could create quite a disturbance as my folks tried to have a quiet scenic family trip. My parents tried to keep us distracted by playing the "Alphabet Game." But we would all get out of hand with giggling and elbowing and sometimes my Dad would say "I've had it with you kids!" and he would pull over to the side of the road and threaten to leave us all in woods for the bears to eat. We would be quiet for all of 10 minutes and than would start up again.

I remember one particular Sunday in July, a drippy hot day, when we piled into our wagon and headed to the Black Hills outside of Rapid City, South Dakota. My Dad was determined to find some red rocks for his project - a new rockery in the front yard. In those days if we needed something from nature we just drove up to the mountains and took it. Firewood, trees, plants and rocks were all ours for the picking. The word "litterbug" or "environmentally friendly" hadn't yet been invented.

As we traveled up hill, winding around the curves, we could hear the music of the rattlesnakes. In the Black Hills the rattlers were abundant and in July they were out and about looking for mates and shaking their rattles. This sound in the Black Hills is similar to the sound of the crickets in the Arizona summers. We stopped at a Snake Farm to watch a handler milking a large Diamondback, extracting the venom into a glass jar. Sometimes we got to hold one of the giant snakes and to this day I love to touch them. After our field trip to the Snake Farm, we hopped back into the Big Blue and headed further up the mountains.

Now we started looking for side roads that might be good rock hunting spots. My Dad found what he was looking for and we all piled out of the car, found a rock to pee on, and then started lifting rocks into the back of the wagon. Yes, this meant the back of the wagon would be full of rocks and the three brothers had to sit on their three sisters' laps all the way home. I wasn't looking forward to this! My Dad was further from the wagon than the rest of us, and all of a sudden he started yelling, "Get in the car, get in the car!" It seems my Dad had uncovered a nest of rattlers while lifting up a rock. He quickly dropped the rock which made the snakes mad. Nothing worse than an angry bunch of Diamondbacks. I never saw my Dad move so fast - he threw the boys into the car, and hit the accelerator all at the same time. That was the last time we got our rocks from the Black Hill Mountains.

September 11th 2001, Tuesday

In September, 2001, we were doing our usual travel as Snowbirds from LaConner, Washington to Tucson, Arizona. This was an extra fun trip as we were traveling in our brand new 2001 Acura SUV, our 1950's tunes blaring on our new CD's, surrounded by the pure pungent smell of new leather. Life couldn't be any better! Also, our alternative travel route had taken us through Montana and Yellow Stone Park, where we saw early snow flakes, fall foliage, and bison. Our mood had changed from the doom and gloom of dark, rainy days to one of anticipation, looking forward to the dry desert and bright blue sun.

Like most of our trips, we planned our overnights in places we had yet to visit. On September 11th Monday, we stayed at the Comfort Inn on the outskirts of Santa Fe, New Mexico. In the morning we had a bus tour planned for the historical district and art museums. This was our last day before the final push through Albuquerque, Silver City, and to our apartment in East Tucson. After throwing our weary suitcases, full of dirty clothes, onto our beds at the Comfort Inn, we bagged ourselves with swimsuits and climbed into the hot tub to absorb the hot sun and sooth our stiff car seat joints. We felt truly blessed with such a spoiled life style.

In the early morning, I loved my sipping coffee with a quick flash of CNN news while Pete took a hot shower. As I turned on the TV, I thought for a minute I had a wrong station. A plane was flying into a tall skyscraper, flames and smoke were slashing through the air, the news announcer's voice was full of fear and horror. "What on earth!?," I asked myself. "Must be one of those horror Sci-Fi movies," so I turned to another news station. Again I saw the same image, a large plane colliding with a skyscraper and it looked like one of the Twin Towers in New York City. I could feel the numbness creep from my toes to the hairs on my head. I carefully set my coffee down and perched on the edge of the bed. Stunned into absolute silence, I bent forward to listen to every word the CNN newscaster had to say. "No, this can't be true, things like this don't happen in my country, not in America." Still unbelieving, I sat frozen on the edge of the bed; then I heard the word "terrorists" and the announcer said the President of the United States was grounding all airplanes and closing the airports. More attacks were to be expected. Now I felt really scared for myself and my family. But, wait Pete was still in the shower and I had heard all this new news all by myself and he was still whistling away as though life was still on a roll. I opened the bathroom door, and said, "Pete, something terrible is going on in New York City. A large aircraft slammed into a skyscraper, one of the Twin Towers, I think. Seems unreal to me, but you will want to see this for yourself." Pete was in no hurry to leave the warm shower to look at another horror story on a news station, but eventually he sat on the bed with me and watched the unusual horrific pictures.

I was coming out of my shock, while Pete was starting into his numbness. After all, I was ten minutes ahead of him in digesting this unthinkable news report. Now we were like two frozen polar bears, side by side, poached eggs staring into the visual images of disaster. To our horror, another plane descended from above and crashed into another skyscraper, causing heavy damage and a falling of much debris, ash, and smoke which made the pictures difficult to see. I had been through the dust storm from the Mt. St. Helens volcanic eruption and this looked much the same. And once again, we were witnesses to people dying before our faces. Speculation began by the announcers as to whether the buildings would stay upright, and during this continued speculation, the worst happened - one tower came crashing down and then within minutes the second tower slammed to the earth like a stack of dominoes leaving no room between the tiles so all ash, debris, and dead human flesh flew into the air. I wanted to turn the TV off and start the day anew. But we were still frozen and the ice was not about to thaw, so we kept watching until more awful images were displayed one after the other. Soon we called our daughters - just to visit as we needed to hear their voices. Family comforting was necessary to all of us.

Later the same morning, we remembered our downtown bus tour but, wait, would this still be happening or not? So we called to verify and found the Santa Fe buildings downtown were closed for the day. Glued to the minute by minute account of the high jacking events, we watched CNN all morning, leaving at noon to walk to Denny's for lunch. Our waitress, a college age girl with large brown sad eyes, seemed overly distraught, so Pete asked her if she was okay. She explained that she had family in New York City and couldn't get through on her cell phone because of the busy signal, so she didn't know if they had been downtown or not. We felt so sorry for her. She was going through the motions of the job but clearly her thoughts were elsewhere. The rest of this horrific day we too went through the motions of mundane tasks while our prayers and hearts were with the New Yorkers.

Sicily, Ed, and Ruffles

In the 1990's our backyard was the Ventena Golf Course and the Catalina Mountains in Tucson, Arizona. We were new to apartment life and the desert so each day was full of new surprises. Our two bedroom, two bath, apartment faced East and bordered the ninth green of the Ventena Golf Course. Privacy was assured as we were on the backside of a large building that housed eight apartment units. Out our ground floor patio door we encountered the most amazing sights on a one hundred yard square, desert wash that included the artistic landscape of prickly pear, saguaro, ocotillo, organ grinder, and mesquites. We really felt apart of the desert wildlife and cherished each bug, scorpion, rattle snake, javelina, bobcat, coyote, grey wolf, and red-tailed hawk that passed by our window.

Arriving in September in 1998 as snowbirds to our compound, we noticed we had new neighbors, right next door to us. A young, fortish couple with lots of outdoor toys were unloading their SUV wagon. We saw kayaks, roller skates, bicycles, and exercise equipment. A person's stuff tells a lot about the person so we surmised this was definitely an outdoor couple. Sicily and Ed introduced themselves and told us they were new to Tucson, looking for a new place to have fun after living in the Florida Everglades. We wanted to know more about them, but politely disappeared inside our apartment to let them finish their unloading of furniture and stuff. Later we saw a calico cat on our back patio and knew this to be a new neighbor too.

Throughout the fall, we visited with our new neighbors and found out more new details. Sis, as she preferred to be called, was an environmentalist and naturalist who quickly found a volunteer job at the nearby Sabino Canyon Park where she led field trips for the school children and constant never-ending tourists. Sis was a tall string-beaned Italian with soft brown eyes that looked into your heart when she talked. She was a 1960's flower-child who never knew she had reached the age of forty. She was well versed in etymology and fauna and was a valuable resource for us when we found a new, unexplained, bug or plant. What a gift to have such knowledge right next door. Sis was also an artist and collected metals and junk from the desert which she welded and hammered into amazing artistic people and objects to display on her patio. She turned her storage shed into a workman's shop to hold all her valuable tools and junk finds.

Ed, shorter than Sis but also dark-haired and thin, was a retired professor of psychology. Ed was at least ten years older than Sis, and had a wife and children from a previous marriage. His family still lived in Florida. I had a feeling that Sis was a mid-life fantasy dream come true for Ed. Ed had a serious quiet nature while Sis was the gregarious child-like explorer. Both seemed independent of each other at times, as they would take separate trips to visit family or travel on a solo outdoor adventure. Their apartment was always full of their projects and no television set. But both liked the computer so they designed an office for their internet activities.

Shortly after Ed and Sis moved in, we saw Ruffles exploring the backyard desert wash. We knew this was dangerous ground for the cat and quickly went next door to educate Sis about the fact that Ruffles was ready food for most of the desert animals. Apartment people did not let dogs and cats run loose. Another neighbor friend, Ellie, still had her cat because she always took it outside on a leash. However, Sis, assured us that Ruffles was not an ordinary cat and had grown up in the Florida Everglades with alligators, snakes, and other predators. Ruffles was a fighter and could hold his own, she said. After going home, Pete and I agreed the cat would probably not last the week. We had heard the sounds outside our window of the natural food chain as the night coyotes fought for their share of the rabbit. We knew the bull snake could swallow a desert rat whole. Bobcats often stalked rabbits outside our window. Oh, well??!!

One early morning as we lay in bed enjoying the pinks and reds of the sunrise, we heard a terrible growling and scuffling. We jumped up and ran to the window and saw a streak of fur energy, first one animal and then another. A bobcat was running after Ruffles. We had windows all around our apartment so we ran from window to window hoping Ruffles would survive. But wait, something strange was happening. Outside our dining room window, Ruffles had stopped and turned around to face the bobcat which was four times the size of a domestic cat. The small cat stood on hind legs with front legs stretched high through electrified fur, lowered his ears, and showed a mouth full of sharp teeth and let out a piercing snarl. The bobcat came to a screeching halt as if "on a dime" and wide-eyed, looked in surprise at his prey. Then the most unnatural thing - the bobcat cowered down, bowed his head and backed slowly away. Ruffles kept a menacing look until the bobcat was out of sight, then dropped to the ground, licked his fur, and sauntered off to play. We couldn't believe what we had just seen and ran quickly next door to tell Ed and Sis what we had witnessed. Sis laughed and replied, "Now you know why we named our cat, Ruffles."

The Slinky Dog

My mother, Lola, could stretch a dollar so far we called her "Slinky Dog." I grew up in a very small town like the "Happy Days Sitcom." Downtown was three blocks - a drugstore, grocery store, Moose Hall, VFW, a church, and a theater. The drugstore had an ice cream parlor so we could get cherry or vanilla cokes and homemade ice cream - the creamy melt in your mouth, eat all the cone taste. We had no Wal-Mart, Home Depot, Toys-R-Us, Costco or Fast Food Restaurants. Bargains were home made, not found at the discount stores. Cooking, cleaning, and caring for eight people on ONE teacher's salary was a challenge my mom seemed to enjoy. Everything seemed like an arts and crafts project and nothing went to waste.

I was taught at an early age to pay for my own things. Lola gave me a penny for each item I ironed. I could spend hours at the ironing board, even doing my Dad's tricky, starched white shirts, ironing the folds as he liked them so he could stack them inside the dresser drawer. The neighbors liked to pay me 25 cents an hour to watch their children, because I was EXPERIENCED. A quarter would buy me a movie on Saturday nights. I always had change in my pockets and I could easily entertain myself with paper and pencil by drawing and writing in my journal.

Most of our Christmas presents were home made or "white elephant." My favorite gifts were cast-offs from my older cousins - a used pair of ice skates, a scooter, or cardboard doll house. Grandma Edna knitted a pair of wool socks for me once a year and today I cannot be without my wool socks. Lola, the Slinky Dog, taught me how to stretch the use of my wool socks by darning the heels and toes. Today I can still get five years wear from one pair of wool socks. My daughters and husband tease me about my holey socks but the truth is I am emotionally attached to their warmth. And when I grab my sewing basket I feel connected to my mom and gandmother. The warmth of the past flows over me, holey socks and all.

When my mom lived on her social security check she opened up a recycled children's clothing store. She put packages of infants' clothing together for the new mothers in town and gave these away. The low-income parents could count on her to help them, no questions asked. She loved to see the smiles on their faces and feel the joy of helping another new baby in town. I don't think Lola made much money from her clothing business but she loved to shop the thrift stores for the bargains, like she did when she had babies of her own.

Later in life, her thrift store knowledge expanded to collecting and selling antiques. This became a profitable adventure and quickly replaced the clothing business. Whenever I visited her in Moyie Springs, Idaho, she would want to drag me to the garage sales and auctions. I had a full-time career going and two teenagers and absolutely no interest in people's leftover stuff. To keep Lola happy, I would traipse along, telling myself that at least I was getting much needed exercise. She knew the valuables from the junk but it all looked the same to me. When she could no longer live in her own home, due to a series of strokes, Pete and I helped her sort through her stuff.

Lola was moving to Arizona and into a small apartment. Going through all her collectibles, and there were thousands of these, took several days. Pete and I would take things out of the cupboards, place them on the kitchen table in front of Lola's watchful eye and she would decide what to do with each item. We had a pile for the antique auction, a pile for the trash can, and a pile for the give-aways. I would start towards the trash can with some stinky, ugly piece of pottery and mother would say, "Diana, wrong place - that goes to the antique auction." I was impressed, although somewhat irritated, with her ability to know the difference. Thank God she was around to dispose of her final antique-junk items. She gained a few thousand dollars for her last hurray at the Moyie Springs antique auction.

There were times in my life when stretching a dollar became my survival. "Never pay first price," Lola would say. The Slinky Dog is always with me when I spend my money. When I was a high school principal and didn't care to shop for clothes, I bought all my wool suits at the local thrift store. The style and variety suited my taste and I could afford more suits. People thought my suits looked expensive but my pocketbook knew the difference. For my retirement clothes, I shop the sale racks at the mall. I have always excelled at finding the lowest price, which becomes a game for me the moment I arrive at the stores. There is no logic here because I can afford first price but that doesn't give me the fun of the game and the thrill of the bargain. Although I love the mall sale racks, I have never inherited the thrift store, garage sale, and antique bargain hunting my Mom enjoyed. But my life is not over and I may find antiquing another game I can't avoid. Perhaps the voice of the Slinky Dog will take me in that direction.

Spilling Over With Heroes

Who really is a hero? To me, a hero is someone who makes a positive difference in the world or in another person. Ministers, counselors, doctors, military leaders, politicians, teachers, and parents certainly have the potential to become heroic. I could list hundreds of heroes who have affected my life in a positive way. So let me begin the journey by sorting out the few who rise to the top.

When I was a preschool child my mother, Lola, was my favorite hero and her father, my grandfather, John Cochrane was a close second. My mother gave me lots of love, cooed over me, fed me and kept me clean. My grandfather fed my mind and had the most influence over me of all the heroes in my lifetime. Everyday he fed my brain with great literature and I loved sitting on his lap listening to his recitations of Shakespeare, The Canterbury Tales, and Ulysses. Dr. John Cochrane had a doctorate degree in history at the early age of 24 and taught history classes at St. Cloud Teaching College. He was a man I idolized all my life. So when I was a little girl he did not read me the mundane nursery rhymes or childhood fluff, but the classics instead. He smoked a pipe. I can still smell his smoke cloud and hear his deep English diction swirling around the room.

In death he became one of my guardian angels, always available in times of stress. As I was growing into a teenager, we wrote letters back and forth and grandfather always reminded me to reach higher for my goals.

Since my real father was never a hero to me, but an obstacle instead, I was forced to look outside my home for father figures - more heroes for me. I always longed for an intellectual sense of direction. Even today, I am still on this mind expanding journey. In seventh grade, my English teacher, Mr. Paddington, was my hero. He introduced me to writing poetry and journals. Everything written down was acceptable to him - he never used a red pen to mark up my flowing paragraphs. I remember writing imaginary stories at this time. Each day we entered the classroom quietly, picked out our very own journal and wrote for twenty minutes. This is a creative writing trick I used with my own students when I taught English in the Seattle schools. And I never used a red pen to mark up my students' writings and even encouraged the non-writers, especially the inner city students, to scribble down their thoughts - all their troubles came out on paper and I think this was a great relief to them to share their frustrations with me. I saw many students in my teaching years that I would call heroes. They were able to make a positive difference in their own lives, despite the lack of family values and safe place to live.

When I was sixteen, a white knight in shining armor entered my life. Of course, in the 1950's all females were looking for the white knight of their dreams. Peter Caple became mine. He was a six-foot two super hero to me. We fell in love across the crowded room - yes, this is true and I wrote a story about our attraction. I needed to feel loved and important during my teen years and Pete's family adopted me as one of their own and showed me the upper crust of life - the fancy restaurants, trips to Canada, intellectual conversations around the dinner table. Pete and his family, Myrtle and Hoyt, were all heroes to me. I felt a real sense of being rescued and Myrtle was a well-mannered, English woman, with a high bred diction much like my grandfather and we became great friends. She was a modern working mother in the 1950's who made important decisions and valued learning. Now I had two mother heroes, one for my well-being and one for my brain.

Now I am in my sixties and I still need heroes in my life. Everyone is my writing group at Maple Hall is a hero to me - it takes true bravery to spit out new ideas on a sheet of paper. Claire is our leader, a perky positive hero, always ready to test her insights of writing skills on our willing brains. She makes us all feel like heroes as we share our story gifts with one another. So here I am in 2007, still looking for my heroes. What will my heroes look like in 2010 or 2020? I have no idea but I do know they are out there and I am excited about stimulating my life with these new heroes who will certainly cross my humble path.

A Summer Spree

We are at a standstill, waiting to board. The greyhound bus has no empty seats. The smell of diesel fuel is in the air. I am on one of my favorite alone trips on June 26th, 2008 out to explore a new public transportation system. It is 2:00 pm and I have been traveling since 6:30 am. I have been on two ferry rides already and this will be the third ferry trip in one day. Quite the marathon, I think to myself. Although I find the ferries easy to travel on. I walk when I like, eat when I like, sleep when I like, do crossword puzzles, and write stories. Riding a ferry upon the blue seas is like being suspended in a large fish bowl, surrounded by all the comforts of home. A suspension of disbelief and pure pleasure.

This third ferry ride is the most surprising to me, because

everything is brand new. The greyhound is waiting for the ground signalman to start the boarding of the tour buses. We will be the first to go on board, as we sit directly inside the huge "Super C" B.C. Ferry that crosses from Horseshoe Bay to Nanaimo. (Cost one way is $15.50 from downtown Vancouver to the Greyhound Bus Station at Howard Johnson's Hotel in downtown Nanaimo, B. C.) I will be staying overnight at the Howard Johnson's on the fourth floor overlooking the swimming pool. (Cost is $60.00 for one night). Off to the left of the bus is a control tower where people sit at computers and mastermind the loading of the vessel. This ship has five decks. The two lower decks are loaded simultaneously; trucks and buses on the first level and cars on the second level, holding a total of 370 vehicles. Coming down the hill to Horseshoe Bay Terminal we passed hundreds of cars backed up several miles. Some cars will wait 3 to 4 hours to board this ferry, but the greyhound, like the tour buses has its own special lane that stops at an open lot directly in front of the second deck. Now we get a wave to move forward from the bright orange garbed deckhand. After parking, we hear instructions from the bus driver before leaving the bus. "Be sure and grab what you need for our two hour ferry trip - purses, books, cameras, and other personnel items. We will not get back on the bus until 20 minutes before our arrival. You will hear the loudspeaker announce our boarding time. I will wait for no person so make sure you are back on board promptly. Have fun on the ferry as there is much to see and enjoy."

A few people line up by the elevator, but I climb the stairs as I enjoy the exercise. I look backwards to locate the bus, so I can place it on my way down for the departure. Looking backwards is a visual trick that never fails me. Once on the third deck, I immediately smell the Starbucks coffee, the sweat of 1,650 tourists, the salt air from open decks, and much, much more. The noises of international languages bounce back and forth. Exploring this vessel will be a challenge, but my Echo walking shoes are up to the job. The name of this ferry is "Coastal Renaissance", built in 2007; it has the latest in marine design and technical advancement and is the largest double-ended ferry in the world. I had not known I would be entering such an amazing adventure when I left home this morning but here I am. Five decks is a lot to explore so like a hungry tourist I head for one of the three full-service restaurants to fuel my engine. Seems everyone has the same idea. The lines are long but move quickly. Having paid for my order of Bob's cheeseburger, I find a chair and table with a 180 degree view of North Vancouver and Stanley Park. The soft blue sky melts into the aqua marine sea, and I am spacing out into nowhere, contended as a harbor seal sleeping on his back. Nothing more fun than this trip across the Georgia Strait on a clear day.

After a full stomach, I stride the third deck, 280 feet long, and discover I am truly on an ocean liner with all the amenities of a first-class hotel. The double ended decks allow for 180 degree views of where you were and where you are now going. The movement of the ship is steady, the engines quietly purring many stories below. The last time I crossed the Georgia Strait was in a 24 foot Trophy bayliner in six foot seas and as we tossed backwards and forwards, my skipper husband, Peter, calmly slowed the engine to each climbing wave and steered us home to Nanaimo. Ahh, Peter, I think I will give him a call, just to see if my phone card will work out here in the middle of the sea. I had located a row of public phones on this vessel next to the computer Wi-Fi room, where business people hunched over their electronic duties. Yes, my MCI phone card worked just fine and we exchanged the usual spousal chat. Peter was quite amazed that I could call from the middle of the Georgia Strait.

As I explore further, I pass by a daycare center, equipped with slides and seesaws, and a large screen digital television mounted on a wall above comfortable leather seats. CNN is blasting the usual horrors of the day and I quickly glance away. I poke my head into the gift store which sells souvenir junk, convenient toiletries, and expensive arts and crafts. Among my other finds are: travel agencies, clothing and leather stores, coffee stands, a large screen sports bar, a work-out center, and large sweeping outdoor decks with umbrellas to shade the sun and small cafes to satisfy my thirst. The top deck is my favorite which gives me a wide-open walking trail in both directions. On the top I could trade the sounds of too-many people for the shrill cries of the seagulls and the smells of the salty brine. This is a trip to be repeated many times.

Sweet Sixteen

Diana sat on a wooden bench at Edmonds Senior High School, smoothing out her poodle skirt which ballooned over three starched petticoats. Her mom Lola had given her extra shopping money for school clothes, as this was her first year at a new school. Lola wanted her to fit in and make new friends. She, on the other hand, did not like fitting in but preferred to rise above the status quo, be more of an adult, like she was at home caring for her five younger siblings. The girls of her age seemed so silly. They talked too much about boyfriends and other trivial things like hair dos, clothing and gossip about the "fast" girls. Feeling uncomfortable in her padded Playtex pointed bra, she glanced down at her brand new saddle shoes, brown and white with little bells tied on the front which was what the sales clerk had said was "the latest fashion." Her tight pink knit sweater made her itch but she kept in control and looked at her Mickey Mouse watch. Two more minutes before Home Ec. Class.

A soft breeze swept through her tightly sprayed page boy. Dishwater blonde bangs were cut straight across just above her eyebrows. Someone was calling her, "Diana, come quick, before I close the door," shouted Miss Sullivan. She hurried off to class. If the door was closed you had to go to the principal's office to get a late slip. This week in Home Ec. the students were studying table etiquette from Emily Post's book of proper manners. She thought this was funny, because at her house if you didn't dig in quickly, the brothers would eat all the food before she could even fill her plate. Meals at her house with eight people all hungry at the same time were chaotic. Emily Post would probably faint dead away. "Diana, will you explain to the class why we have four forks on the table and which fork goes with which food serving." Miss Sullivan didn't really like Diana, because she sensed that underneath the 1956 clothes, Diana was not impressed with all these etiquette rules and often asked embarrassing questions of her like, "Miss Sullivan, what is the proper age to start dating and ride in cars with boys?" Miss Sullivan was a prudish old maid way beyond the dating game and would turn red in the face when asked what she determined to be a "sexual question."

Diana's favorite classes were math, science and English. She was in the college prep classes and on the Honor Role. Getting good grades and competing with boys was her goal - not etiquette rules. She was way smarter than Miss Sullivan and had important adult things to do at home, like bathing her three brothers, ironing her Dad's starched white shirts, nursing fevered brows, and planning grocery shopping with her Mom. Miss Sullivan would never make it in her household - forget the etiquette!

Her last class of the day was P.E. She suspected her P.E. teacher, Miss James, was gay because she dressed like a jock with a short manly haircut. She didn't like petite looking girls like Diana, under developed and poor at sports. Diana always struggled in sports. Half-blind in one eye she couldn't see a ball coming until it was upon her. She reached into thin air to try but all she caught was more air. Taking showers together with her peers was so humiliating. The other girls actually had real boobs while she was still flat-chested. At night when She said The Lord's Prayer she would add, "P.S. Please give me a pair of real boobs. A little more weight and some height would be good too."

Diana spent most of her school day happy because her Math and Science teachers loved her. Her English teacher, Mr. Cunningham, often had her recite her stories and poems in front of the class. Teacher's pet the other students called her. She liked that name. It was her identity. In fact, she knew she would become a teacher herself someday. Most of her friends had boyfriends and thought mostly about getting married, having children, and buying all those machines from the Sears and Roebuck Catalogue. Diana had grown up the second mother of her family, the oldest child. She knew how hard a job being a mother was. Her three little brothers had always been a handful, fighting with each other, and wrecking things all over the house. She had no intention of getting married, and if she did, she certainly was not going to have children. There was talk of birth control pills in the news and that would be the greatest invention ever she thought.

She felt so misplaced in the 1950's garb and could hardly wait to slip on her holey well-worn blue jeans when she got home. Her neighbor friend, Gwen, would come over and they would be-bop to American Bandstand down in the basement. The three brothers would come down and dance with them. She didn't have to fit in at high school. She had her own fan club at home!

Telephones, ETC.

Mable Rucker was the talk of the town. She was a household word. She worked for Ma Bell Telephone Company as the switchboard operator for a small town, 250 homes to be exact. Everyone in Baudette, Minnesota knew Mable. In the 1940's phone etiquette was taught to the children who were allowed to answer the ring or rings on the standard black box telephone. At our house we had a three party line. Three rings was the pickup sound. I was six years old and would answer by saying, "Blume residence." The phone was used for important communication such as emergencies like doctor, dentist, or hospital and for general conversation if important. No unnecessary yakking was allowed.

When we called out to another phone, Mable Rucker would answer immediately when we picked up the phone, "Number, please," she would say. "Just a moment while I connect you." Part of our phone etiquette was to always let someone with an emergency use the line. Mable could interrupt any call by saying, "Please hang up. I have an emergency call." Mable saved lives, she helped doctors deliver babies in the middle of the night, she helped the police catch the crooks, and she could patch together a group of first responders in record time. We all had great respect for our favorite switchboard operator, Mable Rucker. If you were downtown, you could walk into to her office at Ma Bell and watch her work. Sometimes she would let me handle the lines and I felt the power of plugging into 105. It must have had an impact on me because my first summer job at age 17 was as a switchboard operator for a large auto company, Campbell-Blume in downtown Edmonds, Washington. Of course, my uncle Jack Blume, was president of the company so it was an easy job for me to get. I felt so important running the switchboard and announcing over the loud speaker the name of who needed to pick up their phone which was always on the salesmen's desks. I was a cute young thing in those days and the salesmen would stop by and flirt with me. But I didn't mind; I was making two dollars an hour.

In the 1950's phones evolved into an array of colors and the princess line became the favorite. People could have more than one phone in their house and general conversation was now allowed.

The teenage pink princess phone was a popular design and I had one in my bedroom. My Dad and Mom would holler at me, "Diana, get off the phone! I have an important call to make." The phones of the 1950's were so popular that most of my friends had their very own phone in their bedroom too and we could talk away at all hours of the day or night. We arranged for our car dates, planned our pep rallies, and did math homework. I still have a princess style phone in my house and will never part with it.

In the 1980s and 90s, the recording machine became part of phone service. People no longer had to answer their phone; just record a message and check for messages later. This was the death of the spontaneous human voice. As a high school principal I had a phone with three lines on my desk. Fortunately I had a secretary to monitor my calls and when she was absent I had my handy recorder: "You have reached the Re-Entry Program of the Renton School District so please leave your name and phone number and I will call back as soon as I can." On busy days I would not return my call-backs until after school. This was very efficient because I could select the important messages and delete the unnecessary calls.

So that brings me to modern times. Although I still enjoy visiting with people on my princess phone, my husband, children, and grandchildren prefer the modern electronics. At six years old, Sam, my grandson uses an I-pad and knows how to Skype. I have to admit I do enjoy the Skype because I can view my grandchildren on the computer and watch them at play, on vacation, or just keep up with family activities. I had to train my son-in-law not to Skype in the evenings when I am most likely in curlers and a bathrobe. Pete and Susan's favorite communication tool is twitter and they are very fast to receive and send off a message. While I on the other hand leave phone messages that are not listened to for days if not weeks. I don't know if I'll ever get to the tweet, twitter, or I-pad stage of life. I still like the sound of the human voice.

Teen Twist

My mother Lola had a baby every three years. Planned

Parenthood didn't exist in the 40's and 50's. My father Les was a traveling salesman. This is not a joke! Diana, that's me, had a busy teenage life, trying to balance homework, puberty, and home life which of course included much care of the siblings. And care of my mother, whose main occupation was watching quiz shows, soap operas, smoking three packs of cigarettes a day and having babies. Ignorance is bliss and I was a strong-willed teen, who enjoyed all the multi-tasking required of the oldest child in a family of eight.

Lana Turner was my idol although Lana Turner I was not. In high school I was not the type that turned the boys on. I excelled in mathematics which was both my strength and my curse. Boys tended to avoid the smart types. Also, I was boob-less, weighed 95 pounds, a height of five feet, and I definitely was "NOT EASY." We all knew who the easy girls were in high school; they were the ones who got dates, got pregnant, and dropped out of school. I certainly was afraid to let that happen to me, especially since my after school chores included diaper changing, cleaning my brothers' rooms, and lots of babysitting. "NOT EASY" was the perfect place for me to be. And I kind of liked the fact that boys avoided me. I enjoyed beating their brains in my math classes.

Dick Clark was my favorite father figure and had the Pat Boone look that I liked. My best friend, Gwen, and I cherished our two hours after school while we "be-bopped" in my basement to the 45 records on American Bandstand. Gwen and I were risk takers together as we shed our starched petticoats and balloon skirts for the cozy feel of our peddle-pushers. Sometimes we even put bells on our loafers which drove the adults nuts. Gwen had only one brother and her mother worked all day so she loved to hang out at my house, because of all my crazy sibs, and the noise and chaos. I longed for her quiet place. My three brothers and two sisters liked to imitate our dancing as we did the fish, camel walk, stroll, and twist. American Bandstand was the best thing about the 50's.

So Gwen and I survived our teen years and joined the fine arts of fads - the big-hair teased look with lots of hair spray, thick curled eyelashes, pushed up boobs, tight sweaters, and the flirting seductive looks of girls on the prowl. Being geeks still did not bring us any serious dates no matter how hard we tried.

One day our math teacher, Mr. Henry, took us aside after

our Calculus class and explained that we needed to think hard about a non-math career such as teaching or nursing. Female jobs in engineering wasn't even discussed in those days. Well, Mr. Henry was wrong. Gwen and I graduated in 1960 to a world waiting for female and science brains. The new computer industry was on the horizon and Women's Lib was just beginning. So we put the false eyelashes away, burned our bras, and enrolled in Peterson's Business School in downtown Seattle to learn about computers and keypunching. Jobs were waiting for us when we graduated and the pay was pretty good too.

THAD

Teaching high school students brought me into contact with a variety of learning disabilities. My Master's Degree was in Special Education and I had thought I had seen it all until Thad walked into my classroom in the summer of 1980. Thad was one of a kind and so unique that his face and body are still sharp in my mind. Although grossly disfigured he had a captivating manner. But, let me backtrack to the point where I became his student and he the teacher.

In the 1980's I taught Bonehead English in Summer School at Renton Voc-Tech in the Renton Highlands. Due to a lack of campus space, my class was in a dusty hot portable. Despite the heat of July and August, my classes were standing-room only with the most desperate looking students trying to squeeze into a spot. To graduate from their local high school, these young people needed to pass my class to replace a failed English grade. I had the power to make or break their diploma. I saw my job as one of salvage and tried to place each student into materials at a level for success which meant much assessment, testing, and a wide variety of reading and writing levels. Students graduated my class with a P for Pass. Many of these teens had learning disabilities and negative attitudes. I was up to the challenge and dearly loved these impossible kids.

On the first day of Summer School, I greeted students outside the portable with a stack of name tags and brightly colored marking pens. "First names only," I said. "And the first assignment is waiting on your desk. Please start right away." The first assignment was a personal journal essay of self-introduction, simply titled "Tell me About Yourself and Why You Are Here." Students could write volumes on these two topics and also this gave me a chance to analyze self-confidence and writing levels. As I eyeballed each student arriving to the dreaded portable, I saw a most unusual new student who looked like a midget. But as he slowly limped my way, I noticed that he had tragic disfigurements. Entire limbs were missing from a badly deformed body. His large blue·eyes were reading me intensely. He was used to people starring at him and I was no exception. Thad swung his shortest leg up the stairs and dragged his longer leg behind him. Because one leg was a foot shorter than the other, he wore special custom built shoes, one with a sole that was one foot thick. But Thad's upper torso had problems too. He was missing both forearms so fingers protruded from the elbows. On the left side a small dysfunctional web-like flipper protruded from his elbow and on the right he had three fingers protruding from the elbow. His head was lop-sided and missing one ear. Trained to handle most disabilities, I felt that I now was in unknown territory. My brain was thinking bad thoughts, "How will I teach writing skills to a three-fingered midget?"

After several years of teaching teenagers, many with special needs, I had gained a strong survival instinct and quickly realized that Thad had gotten close to graduating from high school so he must have adapted to the classroom. So I adopted a wait and see attitude and decided to treat him as just another ornery high school Senior. He certainly had the teen look with low slung jeans, slicked back brown hair under a baseball cap and the usual unreadable distant manner.

Later as I walked around the classroom and watched over the writing assignments, I saw that Thad had indeed mastered writing with his three fingers and had legible handwriting which was better than many of the other students. I also noticed that his peers from Hazen High School were quite fond of him and he could handle joking and the usual teen-age nonsense. His attitude toward me, the teacher enemy, was the normal teenage Bonehead Summer School manner of "I don't want to be here!" I quickly realized that midget Thad could be mischievous Thad if I let my guard down. Of course the rest of the students were sizing me up to see how I was going to handle the class and what kind of attention would I be giving to Thad. My instincts said that Thad could handle himself well in the classroom without any additional help from me and his greatest need was to be treated like the others. After two hours of reluctant learning from my new Bonehead group, the students descended the stairs and headed to the parking lot. I stood outside and watched the teens climb noisily into their hot rods. Thad had a classic Camero, bright blue, custom built for his legs, and his three fingers clasped the steering wheel with an experienced grip. I, the teacher, had witnessed a new lesson in adaptation.

(Note: Later that day I read Thad's journal and he explained his history to me. He was a Thalidomide Survivor, born to a Canadian mother in the 1960's.)

The Townsend Club

While attending my writing class at Maple Hall in LaConner, Washington, I met Roberta Nelson, one of the local historians from the Nelson-Moore pioneer families. From time to time Roberta would give me treasurers from the past, such as Milo Caple's billy club that he used when walking the streets of LaConner as a policeman in the 30's and 40's. I also have a pair of Milo's hand cuffs and a double circle quilt that his wife, Cora, pieced together from flour-sack cottons in the 30's. One day Roberta gave me a Townsend Club dance card, signed by Mrs. M. J. Caple (women in the early 19th century were called by their husband's name, not their first name, such as Cora.) Naturally, my curiosity was aroused, so I decided to research the Townsend Club at the LaConner Museum's research library. I found many social articles about this club on microfiche in The Puget Sound Mail Newspapers, starting with 1938 to 1945. (Two articles, titled "Townsend Club Holds Big Meeting" and "Townsend Notes")

Curiosity took me into the Internet Explorer to look up the

name of Doctor Francis E. Townsend. What a famous pioneer he turned out to be! "In 1933, he proposed a scheme whereby the Federal Government would provide every person over age sixty a 200 dollar monthly pension. Townsend claimed that his Old Age Revolving Pension Plan could be financed by a Federal Tax on commercial transactions. The plan obtained a great deal of support and by 1935 his Townsend Club had over five million members." (Quote from the book: The New Deal by Ronald Edsforth)

I am wondering how the history books I grew up with had never mentioned Townsend, but I really can't remember all the history books I read and studied so perhaps he was included. My search on the internet continued and added to my short essay. I am choosing not to copy all this data but rather to refer it directly to the reader. However, with the dance card from Cora Caple, I can see the thread of history from the 30's into the present day. After writing many stories about my past and present, it has been a challenge to write about a time when I did not exist. I am now further challenged to write more trivia about the 30's and 40's. Sort of like going on an archeological dig. As I read through the Puget Sound Mail newspapers of the past, I am thinking of Cora Caple selling her dance card for 50 cents a dance to raise money for the Townsend Club. Her little dancing feet helped pave the way to my Social Security check.

Tuesdays with Joann

March 20, 2012:

I got the call - you-know - the call that no one wants to get! On the phone was Theresa's trembling voice telling me her mother, Joann, was in the Swedish Hospital after suffering several strokes. "Oh, no!" I kept saying over and over. Joann was my very best friend; we had raised our children together, traveled together, had lunch together every month, talked on the phone regularly and truly loved each other as close friends do. I mustered my tearful courage, and replied to Theresa, "How are you doing? Is there anything I can do to help?" "You were on my list to call," she said, "and I will keep

you in the loop, letting you know where Joann will be. She had bleeding on both sides of her brain. She cannot walk or talk. We will be moving her to a recovery center and I will call you again and keep you informed." In my shock, I hung up the phone and walked down the hall to find Peter, my rock, for an all-knowing hug.
March 27, 2012:

Another call from Theresa. Joann had gotten worse. The doctors were unable to stop the strokes, as she was unresponsive to the medicines. No progress had occurred from speech therapy and physical therapy. Her daughters were told to look for a long-term assisted living dementia care facility. Joann was disorientated, suffered memory loss, and was incontinent.

I was still having a hard time wrapping my brain around all this difficult information. Joann had been the hardy athletic type. She had climbed all the mountains in Washington State, including Mount Rainier. L.A. Fitness was her favorite hangout - she lifted weights, used work-out machines, and had followed a strict vegetarian diet- lots of tofu and grains. She went through a divorce in the 90's from an alcoholic husband and had lived by herself in a posh condo in Renton Highlands. When her ex-husband died, she took his Jack Russell dog "Sweet-pea" as her companion. The dog was an undisciplined "holy-terror" but through love and discipline she gradually got the dog under-control. Joann was at the prime of her retirement life at age 69. We had celebrated her last birthday on leap year day, February 29th, 2012 at a luncheon at the "Delicious Plum."

I decided to do weekly visits as soon as Joann was moved. Even if I could just sit by her bedside and hold her hand, I had to do something.

April 3, 2012:

Joann had been moved to Aegis Aging Center in downtown Issaquah. Theresa had warned me that she would look disabled and could not respond to conversation, but she would know who I was and could hear me. With a map in my hand, I set off on the buses to downtown Issaquah. Aegis was a four block walk from the bus center into a residential neighborhood. The complex was eleven acres, filled with assisted living apartments. I followed the signs to the main office to get better directions. I was nervous about this first visit; not knowing whether Joann was in a wheel chair or facially disfigured. My own mother had died from a series of strokes so I had some experience with this illness. The secretary replied to my inquiry, "Joann Howe? Yes, she is in the gated community. You will need the codes to unlock the doors." A kindly nurse behind the desk saw my face go white, so she said, "I'll take you to Joann. I'm going that way anyway." Walking with me, the nurse talked about how difficult it was for people to accept dementia with their loved ones. "Most of these illnesses have no explanation," she was saying. "I think she is still in the exercise class." After crossing through the 8 foot tall fence, through a heavy gate that required a five digit code to open, we came to a locked door on the front of a building called a cottage, named "Fir." Joann was seated in a chair doing simple arm exercises. The nurse said, "There is a visitor for you Joann. Would you like to go back to your apartment?" "Yes," said Joann as she rose out of her chair and her tears began to fall. With the nurse holding on to her on one side and me on the other Joann started the slow shuffle walk down the sidewalk. Her stance was unsteady but she could walk and I was grateful for that. After the nurse left, Joann cried on my shoulder and I cried too. I think we were both crying over her illness but also over the loss of all the things we could no longer do together - the trips to Canada, the lunches at Bellevue Square, the hikes on the Issaquah mountains, etc.

I was glad I had come for this visit with her. We both felt comforted. She could not put her words into sentences, but she could say yes, no, okay, and "I don't remember." She knew who I was and listened intently as I told her about all my latest family news. Then we walked around her apartment, looking at her beautiful outdoor photos that she had taken herself and talked about what we were looking at. She could recall some places and other places were an "I don't remember" answer. Running out of things to talk about, I suggested we go for a walk inside the building. After we got to the dining room, I saw some panic on her face and realized she felt lost. She leaned on me and I guided her back to her apartment. Teresa, Joann's oldest daughter had done a wonderful job of moving Joann's favorite furniture and pictures into a small space. I knew this space would be Joann's sanctuary until the day she died. When I said, "I have to go now," she started crying. Walking back to the bus stop, I cried off and on. I cried off and on for the next three days, mourning the loss of my best friend and feeling this was such an unfair happening. Later that week, I received a letter from her family describing her TIA brain disease and giving suggests for what we can do to help her when we visit. Her family too is grieving for the lost mother and grandmother.

April 10, 2012:

Theresa had called me the night before to say Joann had visitors coming Tuesday morning, her stepmother and stepsister. We were all going to the Boarding House in Issaquah for lunch. Theresa couldn't come because she had to work. She warned me that this was the first visit for the relatives. I got the message as the first visit is the most shocking, but this was my second visit and I was now beyond tears.

I arrived at 10:00 am, my usual time, to find Joann sitting on the edge of her bed, dressed and ready to go to lunch. Lunch wouldn't be until noon so we watched the "View" on tv and chatted off and on. I noticed Joann's vocabulary had increased in just one week and she could actually say short sentences. She had been taking a new memory drug. Maybe this new drug is helping her, I am thinking. Around 11:00 am, Joann became anxious about the relatives not arriving on time. She asked me to go to the main office and leave a message that we have walked over to the Boarding House. On my way to the office I see Betty, Joann's stepmother, walking toward me with a pot of tulips in her hand. She was a well-groomed senior, a little stocky, with a cheerful lit up face. Her daughter, Sharon, was parking the car by the "gated community" so Betty and I walked together. I had the number codes to open the gate, so I led them through to the main entrance of the cottage. I knew they were nervous like I had been the week before, not knowing what to expect. When we entered the living room, I started laughing as Joann had tried to eat a chocolate Easter bunny and had chocolate drippings all over her face. "I can't leave you for five minutes, without you getting into trouble," I said. "Let's go to the bathroom and clean up." Betty and Sharon stood in the living room to adjust to this environment - three large sofas facing a large screen tv. The sofas were filled with people at various stages of dementia. One very elderly lady had her head bowed down on her chest and seemed to be only physically present. One man with a smile said, "Hi, ladies, bet you are going for lunch today." Joann's visitors smiled, recovering from their shock, and said, "Yes we are." Having removed the chocolate bunny from Joann's checks, I held her hand and off we went to Sharon's car to escape the caged up cottage. Freedom had never felt so good! Lunch was a pleasant affair. Three of us talked and Joann mostly listened but then occasionally chimed in with a short sentence like "That's nice." She understood most of our conversations, but sometimes would look off to the distant as if her mind was taking her elsewhere. After lunch, Joann walked around the table and grabbed my hand. I knew she didn't know how to get back to the parking lot. We held hands all the way to the car and I helped her get settled into the front seat. She had walked with a shuffle and limp as the last series of silent strokes in her brain had attacked her walking ability. She absolutely had no idea how to get back to Aegis so I gave Sharon the directions and off we went. At Aegis I said goodbye to Joann and said I would return in two weeks. Sharon took Joann by her hand and headed towards her room. Betty followed. I headed outdoors into freedom and a four block walk to the bus stop. I was grateful for the stolen time with a dear friend.

April 24, 2012:

From the corner of my eye I saw the white paper blowing in the wind. My heart rate increased as I dashed after my beloved piece of paper. On the front page of this brochure of Aegis was a picture of my friend Joann and her grandchildren at Easter time. Each time I caught up with the paper, the wind would swirl it away, up in the air and over the curb. Finally I nailed the paper down with my hiking boot, careful not to step on her photo. As I sat on the Everett bus 90X on my way to Mt. Vernon, my heart rate returned to normal. I asked myself why had I gotten so upset over a simple piece of paper. But I knew why - My friend Joann's life had gone out of control like the paper in the wind and I was frantic to capture the paper and return it neatly folded into my pocket. My panic was due to the anger I was feeling over having my dearest lifetime friend locked up in an Alzheimer's facility. My emotions had gone from sad to anger. I had lost my friend to a dreadful disease. Capturing that piece of paper helped me feel I still had a piece of Joann if only a photograph that looked like a normal grandmother with her grandchildren.

Earlier that morning I had signed Joann out of the facility to take her shopping with me at the nearby Target store, and then out to lunch at Chipotles. We looked like a normal elderly couple walking around, except Joann liked to hold my hand for security. She had an intense fear of getting lost. And of course, I had the fear of losing her. As she browsed through the clothing racks at Target, she was her old self, commenting on the new styles, what she liked and what she didn't like. I kept a close eye on her like I do with my granddaughter who is six years old. At Chipotles we ordered giant burritos and sat in silence while devouring all the messy ingredients. Joann does not talk when she eats. Doing one task at a time seems all she can manage. But as old friends, we are both comfortable with the silence. When we return to the cottage we found two desserts waiting for us, our favorite - carrot cake. When it was time for me to leave, Joann teared up, but then quickly recovered, smiled, and said, "Let me walk you to the front door." At the front door I punched in the number code which opened the door. I was free to walk to the bus stop. I was appreciating the simple things of life these days.

July 10, 2012:

As usual I sent a card to Joann asking her to save the July date for a lunch and shopping outing. Also, I phoned her two days before the lunch date to remind her I was coming. The trip by bus from Mt. Vernon to Issaquah required three express buses for a total of three hours. I left at 6:30 am and arrived at 9:30 am. Joann said she would be at the neighborhood spa and massage salon and I could meet her there so I did. One of her care takers was sitting in the waiting room so I introduced myself. I assured her I would bring Joann back to her cottage after lunch and would stay with her at all times. After Joann's one hour massage, she arrived to the waiting room; we hugged and headed out to the freedom of exploration that we both so dearly love. We found the12th Ave. St. Cafe, a 1950's style diner, and settled into a booth to scan the menu. Joann ordered an omelet with toast; I ordered the potato soup and a salad. The usual conversation covered the latest family news, her daughters and then my daughters, her grandchildren, then my grandchildren. As lifelong friends, we never run out of conversation and the time flies by. Then Joann had amazing news for me. Her daughter Theresa will be taking her to Laconner for a four day stay in mid-August. As Joann talked about coming to LaConner, her eyes welled up and tears began to fall. These were tears of joy as Joann stayed in the Thousand Trail's Cottage every summer and this summer would be no exception. I invited her and her daughter to our house and of course we would dine on the waterfront in LaConner, and hopefully outside on a deck, weather permitting. Something to look forward to and that meant no bus riding for me in August. Yah!

After lunch we shopped at Target for some toiletries that Joann needed. She had graduated to carrying a purse and wallet. In the past she had carried a white envelope with only the cash she needed. Of course, she is not allowed to carry credit cards and I make sure she gets the correct change back and doesn't leave her wallet behind. At the nail polish counter we have "old girlfriend fun" picking our matching nail polish - a sparkling purple color. "I will think of you when I use this color," I said to Joann.

As we headed back to the cottage, I asked Joann which way she wanted to go. "This way," she said and she started past the Target store and behind the Target store where the walking trail goes along an estuary and moss covered forest. At the end of the trail, there is another decision to be made - take the short cut down a dirt road or walk the sidewalk to the front entrance on Aegis. We start down the sidewalk and then Joann stops, pondering a few moments, and said, "No, let's take the short cut." So we back-up and then head down the dirt road.

I sat in her room with her for a short time. Her walls are covered with family pictures and mountain scenes, photography she took herself with hiking friends along wilderness trails. My favorite is the picture of Mt. Rainier in the background off the famous base camp with her and her friends carrying 60 pound backpacks. Joann actually made it to the top of Mt. Rainier, but she told me that the man behind her had to push her the last 30 yards. She had felt numb from lack of oxygen and had no energy. She also told me that she would never climb Mt. Rainier again.

When I got up to leave, Joann said, "But you just got here, you can't leave already." Her eyes welled up again. "I have to go now so I can catch my 2:00 bus." "Okay, I'll walk you to the door." We both hate the walking to door part of the visit. Our emotions are strong. There are hidden screaming voices circulating above our heads. "Don't lock the door," one voice cries, "You are locking up your best friend." "Quick, set her free, " cries another voice. With a heavy sense of guilt I punch in the secret numbers, listen for the click, Joann is listening too, and cross the path to the cage door. After punching in another set of numbers, I am outside the cage and free to walk to the bus stop.

Uncertainty

The six-foot foamy swells on the South side of Whidbey Island were getting uncomfortable. We were experienced boaters and had weathered many storms, ten-foot seas, and rip-tides. Pete had worked on ships and boats all his life and now had the dream job of piloting large yachts from the Puget Sound area for an Anacortes yacht broker. Pete could move 40 to 60 foot yachts around the seas like a pool shark moving an eight ball into the pocket. I was always happy sitting aloft the fly-bridge taking in the blending scenes of mountains, aqua seawater and abundant wildlife which included seals, eagles, whales, and salmon. But this was not one of those times and I knew we should not be out in this turbulent trough. And, not too far away a nasty fog bank was approaching.

John had called two days ago to explain the situation. The owners of a 38 foot bayliner wished someone to pilot their yacht from the John Wayne Marina in Squim to Anacortes. The owners would pick us up at 8:00 am, drive us to Squim via the Port Townsend ferry crossing and give us a quick tour of their boat. The 80 year old captain had fallen into poor health and difficult financial times. His dream of living on this custom built yacht in the Northwest upon his retirement was not working out. His yacht only had 40 hours on the hour meter and now was going up for sale. After arriving to Squim on a blue sky summer day, we did get the boat tour and were greatly impressed with the interior design - plush carpets, thick fabrics, granite counter tops, and polished rose wood. As we left the port, the captain waved sadly to us with tears in his eyes.

What a lofty feeling riding high on the fly bridge with so much blue surrounding us. After leaving the John Wayne Marina we entered the Straits of Juan de Fuca which was flat calm like a new-born baby asleep in a crib. The fresh air had a rich sweet smell of salty brine and diesel fumes. We had a thirty mile trip ahead of us and were traveling at 30 knots. As we approached the southern end of Whidbey Island, the seas abruptly changed and we now had a familiar challenge in a not-so familiar boat. When we were boat owners, we knew the strengthens and weaknesses of our individual crafts. When crossing the Georgia Strait up north in Canada we encountered rough seas in our 24 foot Trophy bayliner and had to tough it out until land was once again in sight. Our little boat did a miraculous job of handling the wind, waves and storm but this was definitely an uncertain situation. We did not know how this yacht would do in the rough current and strong wind. The side to side motion was the worst and we realized we had a top heavy boat. Pete slowed down to 5 knots and we rode the six -foot waves, up and down, side to side, like a slowed-down roller coaster. When things tum ugly sometimes even worse things can happen and here it was - a thick fog bank whipping towards us, looking like a smoky smothering cloud narrowing down on its prey. We had no radar on this new vessel so we were praying this would be a fog with some visibility. The smell of fog enveloping a vessel is like breathing in a poisonous mildew that thickens with every breath. The fog seemed to last forever although it was only about one hour. We could see about 20 feet ahead of the bow, not enough space to stop for a deadhead or floating log, but enough space to see another vessel.

Pete always brought his own hand-held GPS system so we were safe with our navigating skills and soon arrived at the northern side of Whidbey and magically cruised through the fog to clear blue water and clear blue sky. Anacortes was a welcoming site and the boatyard even more so. We were glad to have this journey over. Later Pete talked to John about the poor motion of the vessel in the swells and how she had teetered from side to side in an unbalanced state. Something was wrong with the design of this bayliner and Pete recommended it not be sold until it was sea-trialed and reinforced. This was not a yacht that would be safe for Northwest boaters as we well knew.

Unlikely Friendship

Monday, Feb. 07, 2011, 8:45 am - As I walk into the locker room at the YMCA I see Pat sprawled on the bench in a bathing suit not yet wet. A frown on her face told me she was tired and needed to rest. She leaned forward onto her cane; legs spread open, back arched, with elbows and large fatty arms holding her steady. She had survived several surgeries on her legs and feet and through the years evolved from the wheel chair, to a walker, and then to a cane. Pat is not a person to feel sorry for as she is a tough hearted farm girl who grew up with four brothers. She has outlived two brothers, two husbands, and one son. The cobalt blue sparkle in her eyes has faded to a sadness that belies her hard life and too many losses. As she spied my bare feet, she quickly sat upright and a smile darted briefly across her face but then settled back into a frown. We have been swimming together for six years now and we did not like each other when we first met. To me she was a crude mouthed illiterate and I'm sure she saw me as an over-educated stuffed shirt. We avoided each other for a whole year. Our swim class has 40 members so I carefully chose the college educated types like me - Barbara with the operatic voice, James, the ex-CIA military man, Bob, the retired physicist, and Ginny, the retired teacher. Pat hung around with old school friends who grew up managing a 20 acre farm like her. She had a loud voice in the pool that echoed across the cement walls and landed on my unwelcome ears. As I knew almost everyone in the pool, I became curious about Pat. We both liked to garden so we talked about our flowers and vegetables and she taught me a few garden tricks like how to get rid of the aphids by spraying them with a soft-soap mixture. As we approach the heavy door to the pool, I hold the door open as she moves in a swaggered gait, leaning on her cane. Sitting in the chair for the handicapped, the lifeguard slowly lowers her into the pool. Once in the pool her movements are the same as mine and we giggle and bounce into the currents.

Wednesday, Feb. 9, 2011, 8:45 am - As I climb down the stairs into the pool I spy Pat off in the distance. She bobs up and down on a bright orange noodle like a seahorse riding a wave. I wave and start my lap swimming while she continues on with her favorite pastime, bicycling across the pool in deep water. I stop and watch her and notice her silver earrings, and slept-in hairdo, a white grey mop of curls that shows her age to be in the 70's. She has not brushed her hair today for there is the flat spot in the back showing a few bald spots. Wearing the usual no make, Pat accepts herself in the natural state. I would feel naked without my lipstick and powder - even in the pool. She leaves her clothes on the wall hooks and her custom old-lady black loafers outside the lockers. Despite the warning signs of locking up your stuff, Pat is content to leave every bit of clothing hanging outside the lockers on hooks. She once told me that if someone stole her ugly orthopedic shoes and well-worn sweat shirt and jeans, they probably needed them more than her so God bless them.

Friday, Feb. 11, 2011, 8:45 am - I am late this morning. When entering the pool I see the three farm gals in deep conversations. Swimming towards Pat, Marian, and Louise, I am careful not to interrupt but to listen. These gals have much in common - 50 years of farming in Skagit Valley, the deaths of their spouses, a love for the soil and everything that grows. All three have no formal education like me but I have learned much from listening to their talk in the locker room. Today I am listening to Pat talk about how much pain she is in and how she took a bad fall yesterday as her walker caught the edge of a rug and toppled her over. Her legs and feet have not yet healed from the past surgery she had in December at the Harborview Hospital. Pat was born with a birth defect and has one leg shorter than the other which causes a limp. Also her tendons in both legs are too short and must be stretched out during the surgery. I ask her, "Pat, are you done with the surgeries." She frowns and says, "No, I will need surgery the rest of my life unless I resign myself to the wheel chair." I am sorry I asked. We all move back to talking about the weather and how soon the fields can be plowed and sown. I am again a listener as I know nothing about farming. Discussions start about which farm laborers to hire and which seeds will be planted. I slowly back away and start my morning exercises.

Vancouver Island

In the spring when the weather warms, I like to be outdoors. I am a niche and cranny explorer who wanders in and out of every place. All I need for my travel is a backpack, sturdy hiking boots, and a pocket full of quarters, fives, and a debit card. For the last five years I have found Vancouver Island to be a cordial and picturesque spot. Traveling by myself allows me the freedom to stay where I want, do what I want, and not answer to a travel group.

Because I love the small town atmosphere, I gravitate to Vancouver Island's waterfront towns. From Victoria in the south to Campbell River in the north, I have my favorites - Mill Bay, Ladysmith, Chemainus, and Namaimo. The two cities I like best are Sydney and Schwarz Bay. All these towns and cities can be accessed by ferry boats and greyhound buses. I always sail out of Anacortes on the Sydney run to start my trip. But, sometimes I will take a ferry from Namaimo across to Vancouver on the bus and then take Amtrak from Vancouver to Mt. Vernon to travel home.

Fresh caught fish is plentiful at the local restaurants and at dubious shacks along the docks. In Nanaimo, I can sit at a table that overlooks Newcastle Island and a long dock that serves as a landing for the many seaplanes that come and go. The Howard Johnson's Inn has great access to the town. From the hotel I can hike along a brick seawall that has been built along the new condos and seaside shops. The two mile trail goes by a swimming beach, the fishing ports, and into the downtown city area. I can walk up the hill into the city-like shops and buildings, past the railroad tracks, and back around the the backside of Howard Johnson's. The ground floor of this hotel is the greyhound bus station. Once in Nanaimo, I can plan a trip around the island by bus.

Sydney is another hiking place that gives me lots of choices. I like to stay at the Cedarwood Inn which is a six block walk from the ferry dock, six blocks to downtown, and a metro covered bus stop. From here I can travel South, North or West for a low fee of a few quarters. Victoria and Buchard Gardens are 20 minute rides on the red double-decker bus. The bus traveling north will take me to Schwarz Bay which will access ferryboats all along the inside passage, the gulf islands and across to Vancouver.

The farthest north I have been on Vancouver Island is Campbell River back in 1998. Pete and I had taken the month of August to live aboard our 24 foot fishing boat. We had cruised to Desolation Sound, Princess Louisa, Toba Inlet, and the Octopus Islands without incident and were traveling home via the Vancouver Island inside passage. Leaving Quatra Bay, winding around the small islands north of Campbell River in the Georgia Strait, we were in no hurry to get home. Listening to the Coast Guard radio reports, we were warned to seek port due to gale force winds descending rapidly into Campbell River. We headed quickly toward safe waters. Our Trophy power boat could ride above the waves at 30 knots so we passed many vessels also heading towards the same port at Campbell River.

Even the tankers, ferry boats, and cruise ships were seeking shelter. Luckily we squeezed our small 24' Trophy, named "One-on" into an inside spot behind an Alaska fishing vessel and across from the reserved spot for the Coast Guard vessels. We secured our lines, extra tight, and kept the Coast Guard station to listen to the storm warnings. Inside the bay the white caps topped two feet, so our small vessel rocked and while we had a bird's eye view of the Coast Guard rescue boats.

All through the night the 25 foot Coast Guard zodiac left the dock for the stormy seas to rescue a vessel in trouble. We heard the sirens, the blare of three HP Honda engines and saw the athletic crew run down the dock, with emergency gear in one hand and survival suits in the other. The vessel left the dock at high speed just as they jumped on board. With our noses pressed tightly to the windows and the radio blaring we watched all night long. Our noses were ice cold, our hands frozen, but we did not care. The whistling wind, the zodiac engines, and the lap of violent waves crashing over the dock kept us awake all night, as we watched the brave Coast Guard people respond to emergencies. In the morning, the eerie calm allowed us to head out on the open seas. We had never seen so many boats crowded together on one dock, some were tied together triple wide. We were glad to enter the calmer waters of the Gulf Islands, the San Juan Islands, and finally the La Conner slough. Home was a welcome sight.

Vancouver, British Columbia

The Amtrak Train #510 arrived slowly to Main Station at Vancouver, B.C. The conductor announced to us that the business class would detrain first, followed by first class, and then finally coach. Each car would be emptied one at a time. Peter and I were traveling in coach but we knew a secret trick. As the people in coach formed a long line through the cars, we grabbed our back packs (we always traveled light) and walked backwards through the dining car, bistro, and out the side entrance to follow behind first class. We hated waiting for all the people who traveled with too much luggage. As we lined up for customs, we were only 30 persons back, but behind us a sea of 200 people were struggling with their awkward stacks of suitcases, baby strollers, and picnic coolers. We have less than a ten minute wait for the Custom's Officer. Less than a 20 second check of our passports and a few brief questions - "What is your purpose for this trip? Where are you staying? When do you return?" Leaving Main Station, our noses go into shock - the ozone odors are pungent and mired with unhealthy mist, dirt, and gases from a city too crowded with automobiles and towering condos. We instantly miss the clean smells of Skagit Valley.

The 16 degree crispy air bites our cheeks and noses, as we head across the park and up to the sky train station. It was also cold in LaConner early in the morning so we had dressed warm with long underwear, snow boots, gloves, and cozy wool hats. Winter had come early this year of 2010 and probably more snow was on its way. But we didn't care; we were on a three day holiday to explore the sites. As the sky-train whistled into the station, we rushed through the 30 second opening and quickly found view seats. The doors slammed shut, and the virtual computer announcer started talking to us about where we were going, "The next stop is China Town. The next stop is Granville. The next stop is Burnard." We felt like Harry Potter and Herminie riding through the sky on our way to Hogwarts. Out our windows was the panoramic view of English Bay surrounded by newly built high rise condos. After China Town, we entered a long underground tunnel and soon stopped at our destination, Burnard Street. Like mice scurrying towards a piece of cheese, the multitude of multi-ethnic specks climbed up the long steep escalators to the awaiting outdoors full of ice and snow. I stand behind Pete on the escalator, leaving room for the rushed madly driven worker who runs up the stairs as if on his way to an emergency business meeting. The stiff well-dressed business people wear serious looks and definitely are not on holiday like us. The escalators are full of these mad dashers so we cling to the right side. If you are new to this regiment and dare to spread out, the dashers will cry out loudly, "Coming through!" Sometimes a briefcase will craze your leg so hang on tight. At the top street level we see our escape, and head for the nearest crosswalk. The smells of a bakery, a pizzeria, and cigarette smoke mix together to remind us we are in the high-rise metropolis, stores on the lower level with stacked up boxes of millions of people who prefer living in the sky. We wonder about this condo lifestyle and are glad we have a piece of earth surrounding our house with our own trees and scrubs. A luxury of independence that we often take for granted.

Walking down Robson Avenue, we look for our favorite French Restaurant. We arrive here every year on Thanksgiving weekend. No turkey, stuffing, nor gravy for us. We prefer the gourmet chefs of Vancouver - a haven of some of the best ethnic restaurants in the world. The chef greets us at the door; we sit in our usual spot next to the kitchen so we can watch the preparations. Pete orders a breakfast crepe with eggs, brie, and bacon. I order the French banquette filled with Black Forest ham and melted Gouda. Life has slowed down, we have slowed down, and we are in no hurry to rush through such delicious food. The noise of French language fills our ears. We have arrived to a different planet, a place of great customer service. After lunch we decide to walk to our hotel one mile away. Robson Avenue is the people zoo of who's who. Like a stroll on Hollywood Vine where every shop displays unique models of modern styles - merchandise that says I'm very expensive so buy me. Everything is expensive on Robson Avenue but the Asian crowds dressed in black wool and black leather boots seem to gravitate to these boutiques. Pete and I like to look but we save our money for the underground malls with the holiday sales.

At the bottom of Robson Avenue a brand-new super Safeway store marks the beginning of the international food district. We stop to buy comfort food for our hotel room - donuts, juice, fruit, and candy. Now we only have a six block stroll to English Bay. Still the rest of this walk is a feast for our eyes as we pass hundreds of small ethnic restaurants featuring food from everywhere- China, Japan, Russia, Korea, Germany, and specialty foods like New York Pizza, Boston Bakery, a cup cake shop, and Checker's 1950 Cafe. We have no smell or taste temptations because our stomachs are full. At English Bay we see our four story English hotel, The Sands by the Bay. We check in and ride the elevator up to the fourth floor. The hallway smells of freshly shampooed carpet. A newspaper, The Vancouver Sun, waits on the table for my eager snatch. This will be great reading in the morning with my cinnamon roll. From our room #411, our picture window is another eye to the giant city with hundreds of high rise condos, many decorated with Christmas lights this time of the year. The view mixes the old and new, the poor and rich, the busy and the lazy. Every facet of the city lies below our window. We chose the backside of the building away from the noise of the buses, cars, and chatter that goes on all night long. On the backside we see children having snowball fights, workers hanging out for a smoke or a joint, the street bum pushing a cart up the hill, and a dumpster diver loading up a large black plastic bag. As I lay down for an afternoon rest, my brain is full of the tightly packed ideas of city adventures yet to come. Will we stroll along the Sea-wall through Stanley Park? Will we ride mini-ferry across to Granville Island? Will we go to the IMAX theatre on the waterfront? Will we visit the world's largest aquarium? Slowly by brain shuts down and I am able to sleep. Dreams come and go of a newly found city dweller who looks a lot like me.

The Visit

I am sitting in my 2001 Acura SUV in the garage, adjusting the seat by pushing my personal number two button. Suddenly I smell the aroma of mild pipe tobacco as I am backing out of my garage. "Good Morning, Diana," my grandfather says smugly, "Okay if I tag along today?" Most people would have fainted to hear a voice from the past, but not me. My grandfather was my guardian angel even after his death in 1970, an occasional visit was not unexpected. "Well then, buckle up," I reply. He looks over at my harness and looks confused, I realize he hasn't a clue as to how to do this. I stop the car and come over to the passenger side, open the door, and show him how the buckle up procedure works. "While you are at it," he says, "What are all these levers for on the inside of the door? Where is the roll down handle for the window? Where is my ash tray?" I show him how to use these new gadgets and then push the button for the garage door to close. His eyes widen to see a large double car door come tumbling towards us. He raises his hand as if to stop it.

I realize that my usual day of chores in Mt. Vernon has turned into a most unusual day with grandfather at my side. He wears his usual college attire of baggy gray suit, vest, white starched shirt, black oxford shoes and gray top hat. His silver blue piercing eyes stare at me from under thick dirty glasses. Shocking white tuffs of hair spring from under the hat gliding downward to a razor crisp edge on the back of his neck. A dark brown mole bubbles outward on his left cheek like a frozen pea. Even as a child I had wished to pluck this stray mole off its perch. "My gate-keeper only gave me six hours so I'm yours until 2:00, so every minute is golden," he says with a gentle captivating grin. I make adjustments in my brain for the strange unexpected events yet to happen. Not a great day to have him along, I am thinking, as I have a medical appointment and shopping to do, but, oh well, he will be impressed with the new medical technology. "Sorry," I say, "but I wasn't expecting you and my first stop today is for a Mammogram." "What is that?" he asks. "Well, grandfather, do you remember how the women of your generation died from advanced stages of breast cancer?" "Yes," he replies. "Skagit Radiology has an advanced digital xray machine that takes pictures of breasts that can be analyzed by radiologists as to whether there are pre-cancerous tumors or not. Many lives are saved today by this detection procedure." Grandfather and I were comfortable discussing all facets of life.

Silence sets in on our journey down McLean Road. Grandfather is eagerly soaking in the new sights of the farm land, the new farm machinery, the huge new brick houses that sit on 40 acre lots, and waves vigorously to the school children waiting at the various school bus stops. As we reach our destination, I am glad my grandfather has a universal look. He will enjoy reading the newspapers and magazines while I have my Mammo. He pulls out his pocket fob from inside his vest and notes the time of 10:00 am. I am feeling sad as I like having him around and I know the clock is ticking too fast for both of us.

Later, after my Mamo, Grandfather is frowning on the way to the car and says, "Sure wish I had skipped the news reports. Didn't read anything positive. Global warming, wars in the Middle East, famine in Africa, terrorism threats, and even the politicians are angry about most everything. Is there no one in charge?" "No, not at this moment- it's an election year. Hope is on the horizon with a new president and grandfather, you won't believe this but we could even have a woman president or a black man for president."But, yes, these are nervous times we live in, sort of like the "Duck and Cover Days" of the 1950's. Hopefully we humans won't destroy ourselves through greed and domination."

Moving on to happier things, we stop at a donut shop for our favorite chocolate glazed rolls and coffee. No more talk about current events. " Grandfather, I need to warn you about our next place which is a large discount shop like a warehouse with products stacked to the ceilings. You can push the cart around but please stay close by. If we get separated I'll meet you up by the cash registers. As I flash my Costco card at the entrance way, Grandfather's eyes drift to the 52 inch, flat panel tv screens. "Can't believe someone would want one of these elephants in their living room", he says. " I never liked tv, even the early black and whites." I quickly steer him past the electronic gadgets and to the grocery aisles. "I don't want to be in here all day, so save some of your questions for the ride home," I say. My favorite spot inside Costco's is the frozen section. I linger between the five cheese raviola and the pork egg rolls. "Your grandmother would have loved these frozen selections, " grandfather says. "She never liked to cook." "I know," I say, "I have inherited her genes and would rather do a cross-word puzzle or write a story than be in the kitchen - the most boring room in the house. " We continue down the grocery aisles while I toss more prepared food into my basket - Marie Calendar chicken-pot pies, Swedish meatballs, Tyson chicken tenders, Mexican enchiladas, and frozen Alaska cod filets. My daily diet was definitely gourmet frozen Costco's and I loved it. As we leave I stop at the Bank of America ATM machine and grab some twenties. This really startles grandfather as he tries to figure out how a machine can cough up money and just who's money is it. "Mine," I reply.

Not a quiet ride home, as grandfather asks a hundred questions about electronics, banking, politics, etc. etc. He too has a curious mind and I suspect that is why he enjoys these visits. At the house I give him a quick tour of the latest gadgets - the microwave, self-cleaning oven, Apple computer, and my latest fun gadget - my I-pod for audio books. As I put a fresh pine log into my wood stove, he says," Ah! Some things do stay the same. Remember helping me stack the wood at my place and sitting by the stove in the evening while I read stories to you." "Of course, I do." I smile and gaze into his sobering blue eyes. The pocket watch comes out and chimes at 2:00 pm. The smell of pine burning and the pipe tobacco is all that is left in the room.

Waiting And Watching

In 1966, Pete and I, Diana, ages 23 and 22, had been married for three years. While living in a rented house in the Fremont District, we both worked and played in the city of Seattle, WA. Thinking we were smarter than our friends, who were saddled down with crying, whining children, we postponed our family life to travel and spent money on ourselves and our things. Our last purchase had been a brand new 1966 Chevy Nova, beige shiny color outside, and beige fabric inside. We were Republican, believed in Nixon, the American government, apple pie, football and the American way of life. Our fast spending days came to an abrupt halt one day when a certified military letter was delivered to our front door. Our lives were going to change and not necessarily for the better.

As Pete opened his letter, he called for me to share the news, and we both sat down in shock. He had been drafted to serve in the Viet Nam War. This was so unexpected, as married men had always been exempt. But in 1966, Washington state and Pennsylvania state had run out of fresh bodies and were now drafting married men without children. Too late to get pregnant now!! At first we didn't believe the letter, but after a few phone calls, we knew this to be true and the options became worse. Pete could go immediately into the Army and off to the front lines in Viet Nam, or he could find a recruiter in another military service such as Navy or Air Force and enlist in a tour of duty. Of course, at this late stage in the war, the recruiters were asking for longer tours of duty. Pete's background had been as a machinist apprentice at Todd Shipyard in Seattle, working on large vessels like air craft carriers, destroyers, and Washington State ferries. So the natural choice was the Navy.

Pete's assigned boot camp was San Diego, California. But fate was to interfere once again. San Diego was having a meningitis epidemic so Pete's boot camp was changed to Great Lakes, Michigan. Going to the Great lakes for boot camp meant being assigned to a ship on the East Coast. When Pete called to say his homeport would be Newport, Rhode Island, I had to get a map out to find this location. We had never been on the East Coast and it seemed like a foreign land to us.

When your husband goes into the military, a military wife quickly becomes a number. My number was 392-14-25, which I will remember the rest of my life. This number gave me access to all the services on the Navy base, such as commissary and medical treatment. Pete now belonged to the Navy and I might as well get used to a new lifestyle, which included a very tight budget. But I was resourceful, with my IBM key punch skills and soon found a job in Boston, Massachusetts, where my husband's ship, a Navy destroyer, was dry-docked. "The Charles S. Sperry," 376 feet long, Hull #DD-697, had served in World War II but now was refurbished to serve in Viet Nam. She carried approximately 350 sailors on board. Pete was assigned to the Engine Room due to his marine engineering skills and had adapted to 100 degree temperatures and loud noises. I, the Navy wife, on the other hand, had been assigned to four years of loneliness and much waiting, worry, and watching.

During the four years Pete was in the Navy, he was only home an average of three months per year. Many times his mission was a secret one and I did not know where he was going. But whenever possible he would call me, mostly in the middle of the night, to let me know he was safe and sound, and most times he could tell me his location which included places like Saudia Arabia, Cuba, Africa, and Spain. With my Navy man gone so much, I acquired a life that included my own circle of Navy wives whose husbands also lived on the Sperry.

In 1969, while Pete was in his final Navy year, I got pregnant with Susan Lynn Caple, who became our great pride and joy and also only cost seven dollars. I remember when Pete was on one of his secret cruises, my friend Donna would take me to the Navy doctor for my checkups. Donna was the first to know I was pregnant. I swore all my girl friends to secrecy, so I could tell Pete myself. At four months pregnant, the "Charles S. Sperry" was due home. What an accelerating feeling to meet a Navy ship upon its return. Three hundred relatives lined the Newport dock scanning the horizon for the first sight of that magnificent gray hull.

Someone yelled, "There she is!" and we whooped and hollered, waved our balloons, and started to cry as tears ruined our carefully placed makeup. This was a most special time for me for I had a secret Susan hiding inside of me. Soon the destroyer docked and we searched the sea of white look-alikes to find our special man.

Pete had bright red hair and was 6'2" tall so I eventually spotted him and he was grinning and waving. When a Navy ship arrived, there was still plenty for those on board to do, so again we waited. This was an anxious wait as we looked at the tired, thin faces and hungry, eager eyeballs. We occasionally got another wave but still we waited and watched as lines, machinery, and gears were secured.

Finally, they trickled down the gangplank with sea bags over their shoulders and twinkles in their eyes and we knew our loved ones had come home for a much needed stay.

Pete and I found each other and hugged and kissed and went off to find our car, our 1966 Chevy Nova. As Pete climbed into the driver's side, he said, "Wow! "What is this? Are we expecting?"

I had tied a pair of pink booties on the steering wheel to surprise him and he was beyond speech. His tears and my tears mingled into shared tears of joy. This time our waiting and watching would be of another kind - one of our very own making.

The Water Weights

"Stand by the wall," Judy shouts in her military voice. "Push your body into the wall. Now bring up your knees and sway side to side. Don't forget to breathe." These orders are the same on Monday, Wednesday and Friday at 9:00 AM at the YMCA's pool during our water aerobics class. Most of us range from seventy to ninety but the young people probably couldn't keep up with us. We are the "gusto" Silver Sneakers, exercising for fun, health, and socializing.

"Walk in a circle forward," yells Judy after our fifteen minute warm up session. "Now backwards. Suck in your stomach. Keep your shoulders back. Always good posture. Keep moving." The Y has a warm 92 degree Olympic size pool, shared by the Skagit community and the "Chinooks," Mt. Vernon High School Swim Team. Also all the school children show up for swimming lessons at various times of the year. The walls are light beige tile, the ceiling a stark white with multi-colored flags hanging from the rafters - a cheerful sight with large florescent lights on the walls all the way around the pool. Safety equipment is stashed in all the comers, bleachers are set up on two sides to hold 200 people. Not many people come to watch the seniors exercising, but the place is crowded during the high school swim meets.

"Stand perfectly still. Shoulders back. Suck in your stomach. Body straight and tight. Suck in the air and hold. Now breathe and blow out. Repeat and repeat. Now move your head to the left, forward and to the right. Repeat ten times." Such a satisfying feeling to be in touch with my whole physical being. At age 63 I know my body as pliable and strong. The water is my safety net and I feel at peace in my bright pink water shoes. Water has always been a tranquil place for me, a place for renewal and a release for pent-up energies.

The YMCA is a large white brick building, located at N. 6th and Fulton Street in Mt. Vernon, Washington. The Y's founding mission is still the same - "to develop Christian personality and to build a Christian society." In 1920, a local farmer, Thomas Barrett, willed his estate of $30,000 for capital support of the YMCA in Skagit County. Today the Y building of 20,000 square feet supports a gymnasium, a weight room, cardio equipment, male and female locker rooms with showers, and an indoor Olympic size pool. The YMCA has a proud history and states "We build strong kids, strong families, and strong communities. The bulletin boards in the reception area are full of exercise programs from 6:00 am to 9:00 pm. Currently the Y has 3000 members. Membership rate is 25 dollars a month and an absolute steal for the many activities one can join. But the water aerobics class is my favorite.

"Keep those knees high. Keep time with the music." A fast rolling beat of drums is in the background. Judy stands on the side of the pool and demonstrates the exercises as we start with the frog kick, continue into jumping jacks and rocking horse, cross county skiing, the twist and other vigorous moves. My heart rate is definitely accelerating and my body circulation is a pleasant warm temperature. The strong stench of chlorine fills my nostrils. I feel cleansed like I was swishing around in the washing machine. My brain is in a peaceful weightless no-thinking state. My fellow classmates are bobbing up and down to the music and we all inspire each other to keep moving like a group of ballerinas sliding across the stage. After 20 minutes, we slow down into the cool off time and I inch my way to the stairway leading out of the pool. The stairs are covered with rubber and have railings for safety. I notice the walkers and wheel chairs stacked against the wall. A reminder to me that the water is kind to everyone. I feel like a re-energized bunny dressed in a tropical blue and brown swim suit, climbing out of the peaceful pool into the realities of the day.

Weddings and Funerals

Weddings and funerals are much the same. I have attended a few sad weddings and a few happy funerals. Both events bring raw emotion to the surface where I am able to laugh and cry, feeling emotionally spent and somewhat cleansed as though I had just emerged from a good sweat at the spa.

My first funeral was in 1950, I was eight years old. My neighbor play friend Carl had drowned in the Rainy River. In those days the polite thing was to view the body. Carl lay on a table in his living room, wearing his Sunday best which was a black suit and white shirt, no tie. The smell was a combination of vinegar and lilacs. We gathered around Carl, laid our hands upon his rigid cold body and said our goodbyes. Later my Mom had a talk with all us kids about the importance of learning to swim. Our house was perched on a hill overlooking Rainy River in Baudette, Minnesota. Boy did I learn to swim - the butterfly, crawl, back stroke,etc. I could tread water for 30 minutes and won a prize for the best treader in the middle school. I was a life guard at age 14 and sat in the tall chair on the Rainy River beach. I never forgot my friend Carl and kept a close eye on the youngsters who might wander too far away from the beach.

Funerals are memorable experiences and a chance to visit with relatives you hardly ever see. An opportunity to explore the past of an individual who may have left a rich legacy, been a historian, wrote novels and poetry. Most funerals with the over 70 crowd are called "celebrations of life." I find I learn many new things when attending a friend's funeral. Such was the case with my neighbor, John, who at age 88 had a heart attack in 2008 while driving on

Best Road. His son Dale was also a neighbor and Pete had to call Dale to inform him his Dad was at the Mt. Vernon hospital in intensive care. John's family was Irish Catholic and the booze was flowing in the morning before the funeral at the Shelter Bay Club House and ,later, well into the night for the "celebration of life" get together on John's outside deck. The party was loud and boisterous. John had been married three times and his children, ex-wives, and grandchildren came from all over the United States, totaling 200 plus. Today John's house sets empty, due to his will being tied up in litigation from his previous ex-wives and children.

My mother never had a funeral when she died in 1992. I was with her when she was in hospice care at Tucson Medical Center. Her body was weak, weighing only 80 pounds, and the last stroke had taken her speech and ability to walk. She died quickly, was cremated, and the ashes were scattered on Windy Point high in the White Mountains overlooking Tucson, Arizona. Two eagles flew overhead while we said our final goodbyes and prayers . My Mom had been a creature of the outdoors so this was a fitting place.

This summer, on August 17th, we attended an outdoor wedding in CleElum, Washington. A distant cousin, Blaine, was marrying a local girl, named Summer. We felt an obligation to attend Blaine's wedding, as his Mom, Loni, my cousin, had died the year before. Most of the attendees were from Summer's family in CleElum. The wedding was on the front lawn of Summer's house in the country. Blaine's family came from the Westside and we numbered about ten, as we sat up front on one of the picnic tables. As we arrived on the scene, I felt the wedding stage looked like a "Hee-Haw" show. Picnic tables were lined up to hold 200 plus people who mostly dressed like the Eastsiders do in jeans, boots, and cowboy hats. Wine bottles were abundantly arranged on the tables and people had already opened the bottles before the wedding, including my sister Pam who loved a glass of wine. The aromas from the barbecue were overwhelming, pork, beef and chicken on skewers smothered in onions and green peppers. When the bride emerged from her house, Pete and I gasped. Summer weighed at least 350 pounds and chose a flowing ruffled white satin gown. The first large layer started below the largest boobs I have ever seen, barely contained due to a massive cleavage. Pete could tell what I was thinking and quickly whispered to me - "No fat jokes at this wedding." That made me laugh. Never have I seen so much human beef in one place. The wedding party would not have fit into an elevator. Mother Nature did not cooperate for this outdoor event, a cold 60 degrees with a 30 mph wind that had the table cloths blowing, scattering light weight objects over the lawn. Summer's dress was caught by the wind and I expected to see her rise into the air like a large hot-air balloon. What a mis-matched pair; Blaine was graduating from Central Wa. Univ. next year to start his first year as a math teacher. He was handsomely dressed in a white tux with a white top hat. Summer was a waitress and bar-tender at the Sunset Cafe in downtown Cle Elum.

They certainly don't need a bouncer at that cafe with her around. I felt sorry for Blaine who seemed caught up in an event beyond his control. Perhaps Summer's Dad had threatened him with a shotgun. The wedding was brief, a pouring of the sands whatever that meant. No God talk, prayers, biblical references. Later Pete and I would call this the raunchiest wedding we had ever attended. Perhaps it was a shotgun wedding after all.

Another event I attended that was bizarre and confusing was my daughter Susan's second wedding in Fall City. Pete and I had been living in Tucson, Arizona during the time Susan divorced her first husband, Christopher. Later, she started dating again and two years later became engaged to a man seven years younger than her. By the time we returned home to LaConner, our summer home, a wedding date had been set for December 19, 2004. Johnny, the new-son-in-law was very different from Christopher and I was afraid Susan at age 38 was rushing into a second marriage just because she was lonely and wanted to start a family. At 38 years old she was wishing for a baby or two. Johnny seemed a stranger to me and I had only met his family once. Johnny and Susan had rented a house together in Fall City, where the wedding took place in the living room. A fresh Christmas tree aroma mingled with the lighted white vanilla candles creating a strong perfume of pine and sweetness. Sitting in the middle of the audience, I felt like a visiting stranger. About fifty people arrived, mostly Johnny's friends and family. Many handsome athletic young people sat in the crowd - kite-boarding friends, skiers, and firemen (Johnny had been a fireman for ten years before owning his own tile business).

The minister gave a traditional talk about marriage vows, reading scripture from the Bible. Prayers were given, vows exchanged, rings exchanged, and congratulations to the bride and groom. I was hoping my daughter knew what she was doing and promised to be supportive. Today I have two grandchildren. Sam is five and Devon is four. I have learned to accept Johnny as one of the family and thus the cycles of life continue.

Weddings, funerals, births and deaths all give meaning to life; a chance for time to stand still and be recorded.

Wind Storm of 2006

December 15, Friday, I finish writing my Christmas cards by candle-light. The power has been off for 12 hours. The worst wind storm in 20 years has hit the Northwest. Wind speeds of 65 miles per hour were clocked in Shelter Bay. Friday morning our yard was decorated in green snow but on second look we realized this was branches and leaves blown from the trees. Also sprinkled confetti littered our cul-de-sac as our neighbor left out two garbage cans full of shredded paper. What a mess!

Our nearby town Mt. Vernon still had power so off we go to our swim class at the YMCA. Hot coffee, hot water for showers, and cheerful people are there to greet us. People in Mt. Vernon seem giddy to have escaped the powerful storm. Millions of people from Portland to Bellingham are without power but downtown Mt. Vernon is still ablaze with Xmas lights. We take care of our business - bank, post office, groceries, gas, etc. and head home to the ghost town of LaConner, everything still closed due to no power. On the way back we pass a large tree fallen across the road by Pioneer Park and notice other downed trees in Shelter Bay. The Eager Beaver tree service is busy at work clearing the damage. We hear chain saws and generators in our neighborhood. We arrive to a warm wood stove and our Ben Franklin environment.

Our oldest daughter Susan calls from her home in Fall City. No power there either. She has a coffee drive through business in Fall City, four blocks from her house, which is keeping open due to a generator. She says the lines are long and hopes for a record breaking day. Also they have a generator for their house and with two babies to care for I am glad they are warm and safe. "Mom, if you get tired of candle-light, you can come to our house," she says. I'm weighing out a warm wood stove against two babies in bottles and diapers and I know I've got the best deal staying put. Power is never off long in Shelter Bay - probably one day at the most.

Our youngest daughter Sharon calls from Cle Elum. I hear the worry sound in her voice. No power there either. Her apt. is upstairs above a heated coffee house, but she has no heat in her apt. without electricity. She reports a snow blizzard outside and temps in the low 30's. Sharon has three cats, her babies, and is mostly concerned for Sunflower, her 15 year old long-haired orange striped tabby. Also her cell phone isn't working so she calls me from the Keg Cellar Tavern across the street to my landline. As we trouble shoot over the phone, she remembers that Jeff, her neighbor, has a wood stove. So she takes Sunflower to his place and promises me a phone call later to let me know how she is doing. Later in the evening we hear on KOMO radio that Cle Elum has power. Sharon and her cats will be safe and warm.

Meanwhile we are stoking the wood stove and cooking on the wood stove -muffins and hot tea. Later we will warm up leftover turkey stew from the freezer. We close off the back bedrooms to conserve heat. Candles are brightly lit in the living room and kitchen. Various shadows are casting foreign shapes across the walls and the smells are a combination of burnt alder, peppermint, and cranberries. We sit at the dining room table listening to KOMO radio station. Reports are pouring forth about traffic conditions, delayed airlines, and downed trees across highways. Some people will not have power for several days, PUD reports. Lucky us, we think - we know that the power will come back on at any minute. So fun to sit by the stove and read our books. Pete reads "S is for Silence" by Sue Grafton and I read "The Mermaid Chair" by Sue Monk Kidd. At ten o'clock we don long underwear and climb under a pile of covers. No electric blanket tonight.

Saturday morning we awake to 35 degree temperature and still no electricity. We no longer like the Ben Franklin life. The novelty is wearing off and grouchiness is in the air. The ice in the freezer has melted and food is starting to thaw. Pete finds two coolers in the garage and we empty all our food into our coolers and set these outside on the back patio in the 35 degree temperature. The latest radio news tells us that 500,000 people will not have power for days. We are no longer optimistic about our situation. To prevent further cabin fever we decide to hike to LaConner for lunch. LaConner has electricity and the restaurants are open. We enjoy the walk through Pioneer Park on the new hiking trails across the North side by the water tower. At last, a hot cup of coffee and tasty food. After fish and chips, we head back to the house with a renewed spirit. At the gate house a gloomy note is posted that power may not be back for days. So we decide we can do this with patience and a few trips to LaConner for food and adventure. We settle back into reading our books and at approximately one-o'clock we hear the sound of the furnace and refrigerator coming back on. "Hooray," says Pete. He calculates that we have been without electricity for 36 hours.

Sunday we are still happy about the luxury of electricity. There are many other people in Skagit and King County still doing without. People are being advised to go to shelters if they have no heat. We have been trying to get a hold of Pete's brother Jack, 86 years old, a bachelor living in a Magnolia apartment house. Finally, we get a call from Jack, who says he is still without power. He has been camping out at the malls with friends to keep warm and sleeping under a layer of sleeping bags at night. We offer to pick him up and bring him to our house but he says no and that he is doing fine. He seems happy with this new adventure.

On Sunday, we hear again from our daughter Susan. She is still without power and has been told it might be several more days. But she has a generator both at work and at her home. Also, ten of her neighbors are staying at her home for the warmth. People are making trips to Renton to do laundry, buy groceries and gas. Her husband, Johnny, is making runs to Renton for milk products to keep the coffee stand in business. Susan says Fall City Espresso is selling more coffee that ever. People are buying ten coffees at a time for friends and neighbors. Business is booming!

What a strange three days we have had. We feel happy that people are helping others in a community spirit. We have all made it through the wind storm and are the better for it. Christmas time this year has really become a true giving experience and an appreciation for the simple things of life - heat, hot water, and a telephone.